North African Recipes

Moroccan Recipes, Algerian Recipes, Tunisian Recipes and More in One Delicious African Cookbook

By
BookSumo Press
All rights reserved

Published by
http://www.booksumo.com

LEGAL NOTES

All Rights Reserved. No Part Of This Book May Be Reproduced Or Transmitted In Any Form Or By Any Means. Photocopying, Posting Online, And / Or Digital Copying Is Strictly Prohibited Unless Written Permission Is Granted By The Book's Publishing Company. Limited Use Of The Book's Text Is Permitted For Use In Reviews Written For The Public.

Table of Contents

Saucy Moroccan Meatballs Tagine 7

Herbed Grilled Chicken Breasts 8

Spicy Salmon Fillets 9

Casablanca Chicken 10

Moroccan Lamb Stew 11

Zesty Carrot Salad 12

Span-roccan Tilapia Stew 13

Traditional Quick Moroccan Couscous 14

Moroccan Rack of Lamb 15

Moroccan Lamb Chops 16

Traditional Peas Tagine 17

Moroccan Chicken and Raisins Stew 18

Sweet Potato Chickpea Stew 19

Aubergine Stew 20

Moroccan Vegetable Casserole 21

Moroccan Kofta Kabobs 22

Marrakech Cauliflower Beef Stew 23

Hearty Artichokes Stew 24

Basmati Pilaf 25

Vegan Veggies Stew 26

Full Moroccan Dinner 27

Zesty Pimento Chicken 28

Kalamata and Currents Tagine 29

Moroccan Veggie Skillet 30

Chili Squash and Lamb Stew 31

Orangy Chicken Stew 32
Herbed Potato Fritters 33
Stuffed Bell Pepper Caps 34
Balsamic Carrots 35
Saucy Seared Tuna 36
Algerian Pie of Chickpeas: Garantita 37
Sweet and Zesty Chicken Stew 38
Homemade Baklava: Algerian Style 39
Algerian Ground Beef and Hominy 41
Full North African Couscous 42
Simple Kisra: North African Flat Bread 43
North African Poached Eggs: Chakchouka Algerian 44
Spicy Algerian Cucumbers: Salatat Khiyar 45
Sweet Semolina Cake: Basboussa 46
Algerian Layered Cheese Pastry: Borek 47
Traditional Butter Cookies: Sables 48
North African Green Beans 49
Saucy Algerian Carrots: Zrodiya Mcharmla 50
Sweet Almond Cookie Pops: Mchewek 51
Full Algerian Dinner: Garbanzo Chicken Stew 52
Semolina and Honey Dessert: Tamina 53
Hot Carrots 54
Sesame Cookies: Helouwa Ta'aba 55
Mini Almond Cakes: Makrout a Louz 56
North African Dinner Rolls 57
Cheesy Beef & Potato Casserole: Batata Merhiya 58
Lemony Roasted Chicken: Djedj Mechou 59

Sweet & Sour Lamb with Pears 60
Alergian Date Appetizer 61
Algerian Saffron Soup 62
Algerian Style Whole Chicken with Orzo 63
Algerian Fava Beans 64
Sweet Algerian Harissa 65
Artisanal Algerian Bread 66
Algerian Egg Rolls 67
North African Breakfast Quiche 68
Algerian Stuffed Grape Leaves: Dolmas Dalya 69
Simply Roasted Chicken 71
Algerian Tomato Salad 72
North African Meatballs 73
A Delicious Stew in Tunisia 74
Hot Harissa Chicken 75
Tunisian Squash 76
North African Chicken Soup 77
Tunisian Lamb Quiche 78
Pasta Tunisia 79
Tunsian Poached Eggs: Shakshouka 80
Tunisia Breakfast Eggs 81
Full Tunisian Breakfast: Spicy Sausage Omelet 82
Tunisian Chicken Cutlets 83
Tunisian Lunch Box: Cucumber and Apple Salad 84
Orange Chicken 85
Harissa: Tunisian Style 86
Lemony Chickpeas Soup: Leblabi 87

Lamb Tagine Tunisian 88
Tabil: North African Spice 90
North African Zucchini 91
Sweet Parsnips 92
Tunisian Egg Scramble 93
Tunisian Couscous 94
Tunsian Sweet Potatos 95
North African Chicken Thighs 96
Plum Tomato Salad Tunisian 97
Tunisian Puff Pastry: Brik 98
Tunisian Couscous Breakfast: Farka 99
Za'atar: Moroccan Spice Mix 100
Ras el Hanout: Moroccan Spice Mix 101

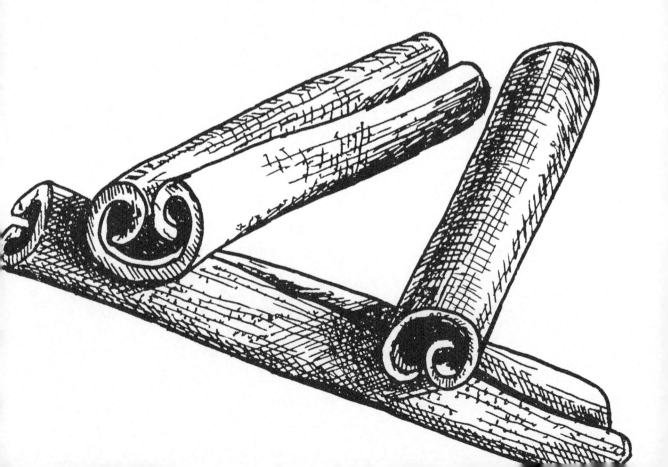

Saucy Moroccan Meatballs Tagine

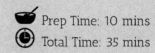

Prep Time: 10 mins
Total Time: 35 mins

Servings per Recipe: 2
Calories   780.1
Fat   59.6g
Cholesterol   136.0mg
Sodium   166.0mg
Carbohydrates   22.1g
Protein   42.5g

Ingredients

Sauce:
6 - 8 medium tomatoes, cored and roughly chopped
1 tbsp paprika
1 tsp cumin
1/2 tsp cayenne pepper
3 - 4 tbsp chopped fresh flat-leaf parsley
2 garlic cloves, minced
Salt & freshly ground black pepper, to taste
1/4 C. vegetable oil

Meat:
400 g ground beef
1 tbsp paprika
1 tsp cumin
1/2 tsp cayenne pepper
3 - 4 tbsp chopped fresh flat-leaf parsley
2 garlic cloves, minced
Salt & freshly ground black pepper, to taste

Directions

1. Stir the tomato with paprika, cumin, cayenne pepper, parsley, garlic, a pinch of salt and pepper in a tagine or large skillet.
2. Cook them over medium heat for 16 min.
3. Combine the meatballs ingredients in a large mixing bowl. Shape the mix into bite size meatballs. Add the meatballs to the sauce then put on the lid and cook them for 12 min over low heat.
4. Serve your meatballs tagine warm with some bread.
5. Enjoy.

HERBED MOROCCAN
Chicken Breasts

🥣 Prep Time: 35 mins
🕐 Total Time: 50 mins

Servings per Recipe: 4
Calories 387.9
Fat 30.5g
Cholesterol 75.5mg
Sodium 725.3mg
Carbohydrates 2.6g
Protein 25.8g

Ingredients
1/2 C. extra virgin olive oil
1/4 C. chopped scallion (white part only)
1/4 C. chopped parsley
1/4 C. chopped fresh cilantro
1 tbsp minced garlic
2 tsp paprika
2 tsp ground cumin
1 tsp salt
1/4 tsp turmeric
1/4 tsp cayenne pepper
4 boneless skinless chicken breasts

Directions
1. Get a blender: mix in it the oil, scallions, parsley, cilantro, garlic, paprika, cumin, salt, turmeric and cayenne pepper. Blend them until they become smooth.
2. Place the chicken breast in a large shallow bowl. Coat them with the herbs marinade.
3. Before you do anything preheat the grill and grease its grates.
4. Drain the chicken breasts and cook them on the grill for 8 min on each side. Serve them warm.
5. Enjoy.

Spicy Salmon Fillets

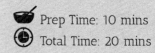

Prep Time: 10 mins
Total Time: 20 mins

Servings per Recipe: 2
Calories   87.3
Fat   3.8g
Cholesterol   25.8mg
Sodium   121.4mg
Carbohydrates   1.1g
Protein   11.7g

Ingredients

2 tbsp cilantro leaves, chopped
1 tsp paprika
1 tsp fresh lemon juice
1/2 tsp garlic, minced
1/2 tsp extra virgin olive oil
1/4 tsp cumin
1 pinch dried red chili pepper, crushed
1 pinch salt
4 oz salmon fillets (skinless)
Olive oil flavored cooking spray

Directions

1. Get a mixing bowl: mix in it all the ingredients except for the salmon.
2. Place the mix to the salmon fillets and place them in a mixing bowl. Cover it with a piece of plastic and place it in the fridge for 1 h.
3. Place a large skillet over medium heat. Heat a splash of oil in it. Add the salmon fillets and cook them for 3 min on each side. Serve them warm.
4. Enjoy.

CASABLANCA
Chicken

🥣 Prep Time: 10 mins
⏱ Total Time: 40 mins

Servings per Recipe: 4
Calories 161.1
Fat 5.5g
Cholesterol 75.5mg
Sodium 574.2mg
Carbohydrates 1.3g
Protein 25.3g

Ingredients
1 tsp cumin
1 tsp ground coriander
3/4 tsp salt
1/2 tsp ground ginger
1/2 tsp cinnamon
1/2 tsp black pepper
4 boneless skinless chicken breasts
2 tsp olive oil
1 garlic clove, minced

Directions
1. Get a small mixing bowl: mix in it the spices with olive oil and garlic.
2. Rub the mix into the chicken breasts place it in the fridge to marinate for 3 h or freeze it until ready to use.
3. Before you do anything preheat the oven to 375 f.
4. Place the chicken breasts on a lined up baking sheet. Cook them until they are done. Serve it warm.
5. Enjoy.

Moroccan Lamb Stew

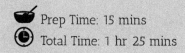
Prep Time: 15 mins
Total Time: 1 hr 25 mins

Servings per Recipe: 4
Calories 764.7
Fat 42.9g
Cholesterol 183.6mg
Sodium 677.6mg
Carbohydrates 42.7g
Protein 53.9g

Ingredients
4 tsp oil
750 g diced lamb
500 ml beef stock or 500 ml chicken stock
2 small onions, chopped
125 g pitted prunes
100 g dried apricots, halved
2 tbsp tomato paste
1 tsp ground ginger
1 tsp ground cinnamon
1/4 C. toasted slivered almonds

Directions
1. Place a large pot over medium heat. Heat the oil in it.
2. Brown in it the meat in batches. Stir in the rest of the ingredients except for the slivered almonds.
3. Cook them until they start boiling. Lower the heat and put on the lid then coo for 60 min.
4. Serve your lamb stew with the slivered almonds on top.
5. Enjoy.

ZESTY
Carrot Salad

🥣 Prep Time: 15 mins
🕐 Total Time: 15 mins

Servings per Recipe: 4
Calories   179.2
Fat   13.8g
Cholesterol   0.0mg
Sodium   95.9mg
Carbohydrates   14.2g
Protein   1.4g

Ingredients
1 lb carrot, peeled and coarsely grated
1/2 C. chopped onion
1 medium garlic clove, minced
1/2 tsp hot sauce
2 tbsp chopped fresh cilantro
1 tbsp chopped fresh parsley
1/4 C. fresh lemon juice
1/4 C. olive oil
1/4 tsp pepper
Salt, to taste

Directions
1. Get a large mixing bowl: combine in it all the ingredients then season it with a pinch of salt. Serve it right away.
2. Enjoy.

Span-roccan Tilapia Stew

Prep Time: 10 mins
Total Time: 1 hr 10 mins

Servings per Recipe: 6
Calories   539.0
Fat   11.7g
Cholesterol   189.4mg
Sodium   929.6mg
Carbohydrates   28.3g
Protein   82.4g

Ingredients
- 1 tbsp vegetable oil
- 1 medium onion, chopped
- 1 garlic clove, finely chopped
- 2 red bell peppers, seeded and sliced into strips
- 1 large carrot, thinly sliced
- 3 tomatoes, chopped
- 4 olives, chopped
- 15 oz garbanzo beans, drained and rinsed
- 1/4 C. fresh parsley, chopped
- 3 tbsp paprika
- 4 tbsp ground cumin
- 1 tsp cayenne pepper
- 2 tbsp chicken bouillon granules
- Salt
- 5 lbs tilapia fillets

Directions
1. Place a large pan over medium heat. Heat the oil in it. Sauté in it the garlic with onion for 3 min.
2. Stir in the bell peppers, carrots, tomatoes, olives, and garbanzo beans. Cook them for 10 min.
3. Stir in the parsley, paprika, cumin, and cayenne, a pinch of salt and chicken bouillon. Lay the fish fillets on top.
4. Put on the lid and cook the stew for 42 min. serve it warm.
5. Enjoy.

TRADITIONAL
Quick Moroccan Couscous

🥣 Prep Time: 30 mins
🕐 Total Time: 1 hr

Servings per Recipe: 4
Calories   448.1
Fat   5.3g
Cholesterol   0.0mg
Sodium   878.9mg
Carbohydrates   89.8g
Protein   14.0g

Ingredients
1 tbsp olive oil
2 medium carrots, sliced 1/4 to 1/2 inch thick
1 1/2 lbs butternut squash, peeled and cut into 1 inch cubes
1 medium onion, chopped
1 (15 oz) cans garbanzo beans, drained
1 (14 oz) cans stewed tomatoes
1/2 C. pitted prunes, chopped
1/2 tsp cinnamon
1/2 tsp salt
1/8 tsp crushed red pepper flakes
1 C. couscous
1 C. vegetable broth
2 tbsp chopped cilantro or 2 tbsp parsley

Directions
1. Place a large skillet over medium heat. Heat a splash of oil in it.
2. Stir in the carrots, squash, and onion. Cook them for 12 min. combine in the garbanzo beans, stewed tomatoes, prunes, cinnamon, salt, crushed red pepper, and 1 and 1/2 C. water.
3. Cook them until they start boiling. Lower the heat and let them cook for 32 min with the lid on.
4. Prepare the couscous according to the directions on the package. Serve it with the veggies stew warm.
5. Enjoy.

Moroccan Rack of Lamb

Prep Time: 15 mins
Total Time: 40 mins

Servings per Recipe: 6
Calories   71.9
Fat   7.2g
Cholesterol   0.0mg
Sodium   196.6mg
Carbohydrates   2.3g
Protein   0.5g

Ingredients
3 racks of lamb
3 tbsp olive oil
1 tbsp ground cumin
1 tbsp ground coriander
1 tsp paprika
1 tsp cinnamon
1 tsp fresh coarse ground black pepper
1/2 tsp salt
1/2 tsp cayenne pepper
3 minced garlic cloves

Directions
1. Get rid of the excess fat from the lamb racks and place them aside.
2. Get a small mixing bowl: whisk in it the spices with garlic and oil. Coat the lamb racks with the mix then place them on a shallow greased baking pans.
3. Place them aside to sit for 1 h.
4. Before you do anything preheat the oven to 400 F.
5. Place the lamb racks in the oven and cook each one of them for 30 to 35 min. serve them warm.
6. Enjoy.

MOROCCAN Lamb Chops

Prep Time: 5 mins
Total Time: 25 mins

Servings per Recipe: 4
Calories   69.9
Fat   6.9g
Cholesterol   0.0mg
Sodium   146.5mg
Carbohydrates   2.3g
Protein   0.3g

Ingredients
1/4 tsp grated nutmeg
1 pinch clove
1 tsp ground black pepper
1 tsp white pepper
1 1/2 tsp cinnamon
2 tsp ground cardamom
1 pinch cayenne
1 pinch cumin
1 pinch turmeric
1 pinch sea salt
8 lamb rib chops
2 tbsp olive oil or 2 tbsp grapeseed oil

Directions
1. Mix the spices in a small mixing bowl. Rub the mix into the lamb chops.
2. Place a large pan over medium heat. Heat the oil in it. Cook in it the lamb chops for 6 to 9 min on each side. Serve them warm.
3. Enjoy.

Traditional Peas Tagine

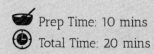

Prep Time: 10 mins
Total Time: 20 mins

Servings per Recipe: 1
Calories   476.3
Fat   24.7g
Cholesterol   372.0mg
Sodium   741.1mg
Carbohydrates   38.6g
Protein   26.5g

Ingredients

1 (8 1/2 oz) cans sweet peas, drained or
9 oz frozen peas
1 tbsp olive oil
1 tsp paprika
1 tsp cumin
1/4-1/2 tsp black pepper
1/4 tsp salt
1/4 tsp ginger
2 - 3 eggs

Directions

1. Place a large skillet or tagine over medium heat. Heat the oil in it. Heat the oil in it.
2. Add the peas with spices then let them cook for 6 min while stirring often.
3. Whisk the eggs in a small bowl with a pinch of salt and pepper. Pour it all over the peas mix and let them cook for 3 to 5 min or until it is done. Serve it warm.
4. Enjoy.

MOROCCAN Chicken Raisins Stew

🥣 Prep Time: 30 mins
🕒 Total Time: 1 hr

Servings per Recipe: 4
Calories   1331.2
Fat   82.3g
Cholesterol   382.0mg
Sodium   1183.3mg
Carbohydrates   57.2g
Protein   88.7g

Ingredients

3 -5 tbsp oil
4 lbs chicken thighs
Salt and pepper
1 large onion, chopped
2 tbsp fresh minced garlic
1 tbsp cumin
1 tbsp turmeric
1 tsp paprika
1/2 tsp cinnamon
2 tsp grated lemon zest
1 tbsp flour
3 C. chicken broth
3 tbsp honey
1 1/2 C. chickpeas, rinsed and drained
1/2 C. dark raisin
Cooked rice

Directions

1. Place a stew pot over medium heat. Heat the oil in it.
2. Place the chicken thighs in the pot and sprinkle a pinch of salt and pepper over them. Cook them until they become brown on all sides.
3. Drain the chicken thighs and place them aside. Stir in the garlic with onion into the same pot. Cook them for 6 min.
4. Combine in the cumin, turmeric, paprika and cinnamon. Let them cook for 40 sec while stirring all the time.
5. Add the broth, honey, lemon zest and flour then combine them well. Place the chicken thighs back in the pot then put on the lid and let them cook for 16 min.
6. Once the time is up, add the raisins and cook them stew for 18 min without covering it.
7. Combine in the chickpeas and cook the stew for an extra 6 min. serve it warm.
8. Enjoy.

Sweet Potato Chickpea Stew

Prep Time: 15 mins
Total Time: 40 mins

Servings per Recipe: 4
Calories   311.3
Fat   4.6g
Cholesterol   0.0mg
Sodium   692.7mg
Carbohydrates   60.0g
Protein   9.5g

Ingredients

- 1 large onion, thinly sliced
- 3 garlic cloves, minced
- 1 tbsp fresh ginger, minced
- 2 tbsp red wine or 2 tbsp cooking sherry
- 1 tsp cumin
- 1 tsp cinnamon
- 1 tsp paprika
- 1/2 tsp crushed red pepper flakes, to taste
- 1 C. water
- 1/2 tsp salt
- 2 medium sweet potatoes, peeled and cut into bite-size pieces
- 1/4 C. diced dried apricot
- 2 C. cooked chickpeas
- 1/4 C. raisins
- 2 tbsp lemon juice
- 1/4 C. sliced almonds, toasted in a dry skillet

Directions

1. Place a large saucepan over medium heat. Sauté in it the onion, garlic, ginger, and wine or sherry for 6 min with the lid on.
2. Combine in the cumin, cinnamon, paprika, and red pepper flakes then let them cook for 2 min.
3. Stir in the water with potato, apricots, a pinch of salt and pepper. Cook them until the start boiling.
4. Put on the lid and coo the stew for 18 over low heat. Combine in the lemon juice with garbanzo beans and raisins.
5. Let the stew simmer for an extra 6 min then serve it warm.
6. Enjoy.

AUBERGINE
Stew

🥣 Prep Time: 10 mins
🕐 Total Time: 40 mins

Servings per Recipe: 4
Calories   175.2
Fat   2.7g
Cholesterol   0.0mg
Sodium   192.2mg
Carbohydrates   35.2g
Protein   6.8g

Ingredients
2 large eggplants (cubed)
1 medium onion (large diced)
3 garlic cloves (minced)
1 (8 oz) cans chickpeas (drained)
1 (8 oz) cans diced tomatoes
1 C. vegetable stock
1 tsp chili powder
1 tsp cinnamon
2 tsp ground cumin
1 tsp olive oil
Salt and pepper

Directions
1. Trim the tops of the eggplants and cut them into small dices.
2. Place a large skillet over medium heat. Heat the oil in it. Add the onion with garlic, chili powder, cumin and cinnamon. Sauté them for 6 min.
3. Stir in the eggplant, tomatoes and chickpeas, along with the stock. Cook them over low heat for 18 min with the lid.
4. Adjust the seasoning of the stew then serve it warm.
5. Enjoy.

Moroccan Vegetable Casserole

Prep Time: 20 mins
Total Time: 1 hr

Servings per Recipe: 4
Calories   305.8
Fat   9.1g
Cholesterol   0.0mg
Sodium   352.0mg
Carbohydrates   51.1g
Protein   9.6g

Ingredients

1 medium onion cut in 1/4-inch slices
1 medium zucchini cut in 1/4-inch thick semi-circles
1 small eggplant, peeled, cut in 1/2-inch thick semi-circles
1 large sweet potato, peeled, cut in 1/4-inch semi-circles
1 large red pepper, sliced in 1/4-inch strips
2 medium tomatoes, fresh, chopped
15 oz chickpeas, drained and rinsed
3 garlic cloves, minced
2 tbsp olive oil
1 tbsp lemon juice
1 tbsp cumin
1 1/2 tsp turmeric
1 1/2 tsp cinnamon
1 1/2 tsp paprika
1/4 tsp cayenne

Directions

1. Get a large mixing bowl: stir in the veggies with garlic.
2. Whisk the olive oil with spices in a small bowl. Add the mix to veggies and toss them to coat.
3. Before you do anything preheat the oven to 400 F.
4. Spread the veggies on a greased baking sheet. Cook them in the oven for 22 min. serve it warm.
5. Enjoy.

MOROCCAN
Kofta Kabobs

Prep Time: 10 mins
Total Time: 30 mins

Servings per Recipe: 4
Calories   500.7
Fat   34.2g
Cholesterol   154.2mg
Sodium   443.2mg
Carbohydrates   2.7g
Protein   42.6g

Ingredients
2 lbs ground beef
1/2 medium onion, grated
2 garlic cloves, minced
1 tbsp fresh parsley, finely chopped
1 tbsp fresh cilantro, finely chopped
1 tsp paprika
1 tsp cumin
1/2 tsp salt
1/2 tsp black pepper
1/2-1 tsp cayenne pepper
1/2 tsp ras el hanout spice mix, see appendix

Directions
1. Get a large mixing bowl: stir in it all the ingredients. Place the mix in the fridge for 2 h.
2. Before you do anything preheat the grill and grease its grates. Shape of the beef mix into a medium log and press it into a skewer.
3. Repeat the process with the rest of the ingredients. Cook the kofta kabobs on the grill for 5 to 7 min on each side. Serve them warm.
4. Enjoy.

Marrakech Cauliflower Beef Stew

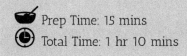
Prep Time: 15 mins
Total Time: 1 hr 10 mins

Servings per Recipe: 3
Calories   935.5
Fat   67.9g
Cholesterol   236.2mg
Sodium   841.7mg
Carbohydrates   15.1g
Protein   65.1g

Ingredients
1 head cauliflower
1 1/2 lbs beef stew meat
2 tbsp olive oil
1/2 onion, diced
2 medium garlic cloves
1/4 C. fresh parsley, finely chopped
1 tbsp tomato paste
1 beef bouillon cube
1 tsp cumin
1/2 tsp ginger
1/2 tsp black pepper
1/2 tsp salt
1/4 tsp turmeric

Directions
1. Chop the cauliflower into large pieces. Run them under some cool water. Place it in the fridge.
2. Place a large saucepan over medium heat. Heat the oil in it. Brown in it the beef for 8 min.
3. Pour in enough water to cover the meat then stir in the remaining ingredients. Put on the lid and let them cook for 45 min over low heat.
4. Once the time is up, add the cauliflower pieces to the pot and put on the lid. Cook them for 16 min. serve it warm.
5. Enjoy.

HEARTY
Artichokes Stew

🍳 Prep Time: 20 mins
🕐 Total Time: 50 mins

Servings per Recipe: 4
Calories　　　　378.2
Fat　　　　　　20.4g
Cholesterol　　　0.0mg
Sodium　　　　470.0mg
Carbohydrates　　46.9g
Protein　　　　　8.1g

Ingredients
1 1/2 C. chopped onions
3 garlic cloves, minced
1/3 C. olive oil
1 tsp dried thyme
3 C. cubed potatoes
1 C. chopped green beans
1 red bell pepper, chopped
2 C. cubed fresh tomatoes
3 C. vegetable stock
13 oz can artichoke hearts, drained and halved (reserve the brine)
1/2 C. pitted black olives, halved

1 pinch saffron
1/4 C. fresh lemon juice
1/4 C. chopped fresh parsley
Salt and pepper

Directions
1. Place a pot over medium heat. Heat the oil in it. Cook in it the garlic with onion for 4 min.
2. Stir in the thyme, potatoes, green beans, bell pepper, and tomatoes. Let them cook for 4 min over medium heat while stirring from time to time.
3. Stir in the vegetable stock and the artichoke brine. Put on the lid and cook them for 22 min.
4. Once the time is up, combine in the artichoke hearts with olives and saffron. Let them cook for an extra 8 min.
5. Stir in the parsley with lemon juice, a pinch of salt and pepper. Serve your stew warm.
6. Enjoy.

Basmati Pilaf

Prep Time: 25 mins
Total Time: 1 hr 10 mins

Servings per Recipe: 6
Calories   168.3
Fat   3.6g
Cholesterol   1.7mg
Sodium   5.2mg
Carbohydrates   31.1g
Protein   3.7g

Ingredients
1 tsp unsalted butter
1/2 C. finely chopped onion
1 tsp paprika
1 tsp cumin
1/2 tsp cayenne pepper
1 C. white basmati rice
1 1/2 C. water or 1 1/2 C. vegetable stock
Fresh ground black pepper, to taste
1/4 C. sliced almonds
1/4 C. raisins

Directions
1. Before you do anything preheat the oven to 350 F.
2. Place an oven proof pot over medium heat. Heat the butter in it. Add the onion and cook it for 3 min.
3. Combine in the cumin, cayenne pepper, paprika and rice. Let them cook for 2 min.
4. Add the raisins with stock then cook them over medium heat until it starts boiling.
5. Put on the lid in the oven and let it cook for 20 min.
6. Once the time is up, season the pilaf with a pinch of salt and pepper. Stir in the almonds then serve your pilaf.
7. Enjoy.

VEGAN
Veggies Stew

🥣 Prep Time: 15 mins
🕐 Total Time: 1 hr 45 mins

Servings per Recipe: 4
Calories   200.5
Fat   4.2g
Cholesterol   0.0mg
Sodium   108.8mg
Carbohydrates   38.3g
Protein   5.3g

Ingredients
1 medium onion, chopped
1 garlic clove, peeled and minced
2 tbsp water
1 tbsp canola oil
2 medium potatoes, peeled and cut into 1-inch dice
2 C. carrots, peeled and chopped
1 (15 oz) cans reduced-diced tomatoes, untrained
1 tsp ground cumin
1 C. low-tomato juice
2 C. green beans, sliced in 2-inch pieces
1/4 tsp pepper

Directions
1. Place a pot over medium heat. Heat the oil with water in it. Add the garlic with onion and cook them for 4 min.
2. Stir in the carrot with potato then coo them for 16 min. combine in the cumin with tomato. Put on the lid and let them cook for 60 min.
3. Once the time is up, stir in the green beans and cook them for 16 min. adjust the seasoning of the stew then serve it warm.
4. Enjoy.

Full Moroccan Dinner

Prep Time: 45 mins
Total Time: 1 hr

Servings per Recipe: 6
Calories   1823.1
Fat   168.6g
Cholesterol   224.7mg
Sodium   325.9mg
Carbohydrates   56.7g
Protein   24.1g

Ingredients

- 3 lbs organic beef, trimmed of fat & cubed
- 1 tbsp olive oil
- 1 lb onion, peeled & quartered
- 4 -6 garlic cloves, peeled & chopped finely
- 1 lb carrot, peeled & cut into chunks
- 9 oz canned tomatoes
- 4 oz dates, pitted but kept whole
- 6 oz prunes, pitted but kept whole
- 2 tbsp honey
- 1/2 pint beef stock
- 1 cinnamon stick
- 6 tsp ras el hanout spice mix (or 2 tsp cumin powder, 2 tsp coriander powder, 1 tsp ginger and 1 tsp turmeric)
- Salt & pepper
- 2 oz toasted sliced almonds
- 2 tbsp fresh coriander, chopped

Directions

1. Bring a large pot of water to a boil. Cook in it the carrots for 4 min. drain it and place it aside.
2. Before you do anything preheat an electric tagine or a crockpot.
3. Stir a 1/2 pint of stock with a beef cube
4. Heat half of the oil in it. Add the onion pieces and cook them until they become golden. Stir in the carrots with garlic, spices, honey and the stock mix.
5. Mix them well. Add the cinnamon stick with tinned tomatoes, dates & prunes.
6. Place a large pan over medium heat. Heat the remaining oil in it. Brown in it the beef pieces on both sides.
7. Transfer the browned beef pieces to the pot with a pinch of salt and pepper. Put on the crockpot lid and cook the stew for 9 h on high.
8. Once the time is up, serve your stew warm with coriander and almonds on top.
9. Enjoy.

ZESTY
Pimento Chicken

🥣 Prep Time: 15 mins
🕐 Total Time: 1 hr

Servings per Recipe: 4
Calories   263.4
Fat   14.4g
Cholesterol   46.4mg
Sodium   423.2mg
Carbohydrates   14.3g
Protein   18.7g

Ingredients

2 tbsp olive oil
4 chicken breast halves (bone in, skin on)
1 small onion, sliced thin
3/4 tsp cumin
1/4 tsp paprika
1/4 tsp cinnamon
2 tsp lemons, zest of, finely grated
1 1/2 tsp all-purpose flour
1 1/2 C. chicken broth
1/3 C. pimento stuffed olive, sliced thin
1 tbsp honey
1/2 C. canned chick-peas, drained & rinsed

Directions

1. Place a large saucepan over medium heat. Heat he oil in it.
2. Season the chicken breasts with some salt and pepper. Brown them in the hot oil for 2 to 4 min on each side.
3. Drain the chicken and place it aside. Stir the onion into the pot then cook it for 3 min.
4. Combine in the cumin, paprika, cinnamon, lemon zest and flour. Let them cook for 2 min while stirring often.
5. Once the time is up, place the chicken back in the pot with honey, olives and broth. Let them cook for 22 min.
6. Combine in the chickpeas then cook the stew for another 4 min. serve it warm.
7. Enjoy.

Kalamata Currents Tagine

🥣 Prep Time: 20 mins
🕐 Total Time: 40 mins

Servings per Recipe: 4
Calories   555.7
Fat   14.8g
Cholesterol   114.5mg
Sodium   461.4mg
Carbohydrates   66.2g
Protein   39.7g

Ingredients
1 tbsp olive oil
1/4 C. chopped almonds
2 garlic cloves, minced
1 large onion, finely chopped
8 whole boneless skinless chicken thighs
2 tbsp harissa, see appendix
1 1/4 C. water
1 (400 g) cans chickpeas, drained
2 fresh tomatoes
2 tbsp dried currants or 2 tbsp raisins or 2 tbsp raisins

1 tbsp honey
1 tsp ground cumin
1/2 tsp cinnamon
1/2 C. kalamata olive (optional)
3 C. hot cooked couscous or 3 C. cooked rice

Directions
1. Place a tagine or skillet over medium heat. Heat the oil in it. Fry in it the almonds until they become golden brown. Drain them and place them aside.
2. Stir in the onion with garlic and chicken into the pan. Cook them for 8 min.
3. Whisk the harissa paste, water, currants, honey, cumin and cinnamon in a mixing bowl. Stir the mix into the skillet or tagine.
4. Place the tomato with chickpeas and olives on top. Put on the lids and coo them for 22 min over low heat. Serve your stew warm with some rice.
5. Enjoy.

MOROCCAN
Veggie Skillet

🥣 Prep Time: 15 mins
🕐 Total Time: 1 hr

Servings per Recipe: 4
Calories	586.4
Fat	16.6g
Cholesterol	23.3mg
Sodium	746.7mg
Carbohydrates	92.1g
Protein	14.9g

Ingredients
- 2 C. long grain rice
- 2 tbsp butter
- 2 tbsp olive oil
- 1 onion, chopped
- 2 garlic cloves, finely chopped
- 1 - 2 cinnamon stick
- 1/2 tsp salt (to taste)
- 1/2 tsp ginger
- 1/2 tsp white pepper
- 1/2 tsp cumin
- 1/2 tsp turmeric
- 1/4 C. fresh cilantro, chopped
- 1/4 C. peas (fresh or frozen)
- 1 red bell pepper, finely chopped
- 1 carrot, finely chopped
- 4 1/2 C. chicken stock or 4 1/2 C. vegetable stock
- 1/4 tsp saffron thread, crushed

Directions
1. Place a large saucepan over medium heat. Pour the stock in it and cook it until it starts boiling.
2. Place a large skillet over medium heat. Stir in it the remaining ingredients. Let them cook for 12 min over low medium heat.
3. Stir in the saffron with boiling stock and a pinch of salt. Cook it until it starts simmering.
4. Put on the lid and cook the pilaf over low heat for 37 min. serve your pilaf warm.
5. Enjoy.

Chili Squash Lamb Stew

Prep Time: 25 mins
Total Time: 5 hrs 25 mins

Servings per Recipe: 4
Calories	553.1
Fat	19.3g
Cholesterol	221.9mg
Sodium	1051.1mg
Carbohydrates	17.0g
Protein	74.9g

Ingredients

- 3 lb packages stewing lamb or
- 4 garlic cloves, minced
- 2 onions, thinly sliced
- 1 tsp ground cumin
- 1 tsp paprika
- 1/2 tsp ground ginger
- 1/2 tsp cinnamon
- 1/2 tsp allspice
- 1/2 tsp salt
- 1/2 tsp hot red chili pepper flakes or 1/4 tsp cayenne pepper
- 2 C. small chunks carrots
- 3 C. large chunks of peeled squash or 3 C. potatoes
- 1 (10 oz) cans condensed chicken broth or 1 C. chicken bouillon
- 1/2 C. pitted green olives (optional)
- 1 (19 oz) cans chickpeas, drained and rinsed (optional)

Directions

1. Get rid of the excess fat from the lamb meat.
2. Stir all the ingredients except for the chickpeas into a slow cooker. Put on the lid and let them cook for 9 h.
3. Once the time is up, add the chickpeas to the stew. Put on the lid and let it cook for an extra 20 min. serve it warm.
4. Enjoy.

ORANGY
Chicken Stew

🥣 Prep Time: 10 mins
🕒 Total Time: 40 mins

Servings per Recipe: 5
Calories   537.2
Fat   24.1g
Cholesterol   66.3mg
Sodium   597.7mg
Carbohydrates   55.1g
Protein   23.4g

Ingredients
Meat:
1 tsp paprika
1/2 tsp ground cumin
1/2 tsp ground coriander
1/2 tsp ground ginger
3/4 tsp sea salt
1/4 tsp black pepper
1 lb boneless skinless chicken breast
1 tbsp olive oil
2 C. fennel, thinly sliced
1/4 C. fennel leaves, chopped
1 medium red onion, cut into 1 inch chunks
1 C. orange juice
1/3 C. fat-free chicken broth
2 tsp cornstarch
1 tbsp water
Couscous
1 C. uncooked couscous
2 C. water

Directions
1. Get a small mixing bowl: mix in it the spices with a pinch of salt and pepper. Rub the mix into the chicken breasts.
2. Place a large pan over medium heat. Heat the oil in it. Brown in it the chicken breasts for 6 min on each side.
3. Drain the chicken breasts and place them aside. Stir the onion with fennel into the same pan. Cook them for 8 min while adding a splash of water if needed.
4. Stir a pinch of salt with 2 C. of water in a large saucepan. Cook it until it starts boiling. Stir into it the couscous and put on the lid.
5. Turn off the heat and let it sit for 6 min. use a fork to fluff the couscous and place it aside.
6. Combine the orange juice, broth and the last 1/4 tsp salt in a large saucepan. Cook it until it starts boiling.
7. Whisk 1 tbsp of water with cornstarch in a small mixing bowl. Add it to the boiling juice mix. Stir them while cooking until it starts to thicken.
8. Combine in the browned chicken with cooked fennel and onion. Let them cook for an extra 3 min.
9. Serve your chicken breasts stew warm with couscous.
10. Enjoy.

Herbed Potato Fritters

Prep Time: 45 mins
Total Time: 1 hr 10 mins

Servings per Recipe: 16
Calories   46.4
Fat   0.3g
Cholesterol   1.0mg
Sodium   305.5mg
Carbohydrates   9.8g
Protein   1.1g

Ingredients

- 4 C. mashed potatoes, warm and plain
- 3 garlic cloves, mashed or 3 garlic, pressed
- 1/2 C. scallion, cut lengthwise and sliced thinly
- 1/2 C. fresh flat leaf parsley, chopped finely
- 1 - 2 tsp salt
- 1 tsp fresh ground black pepper
- Flour, for dusting
- Oil, for shallow frying

Directions

1. Get a large mixing bowl: stir in it the mashed potato with garlic, scallion, parsley, pepper and salt.
2. Shape the mix into 16 fritters then dust them with flour.
3. Place a large skillet over medium heat and heat in it a splash of oil. Cook in it the patties until they become golden brown on each side.
4. Serve your potato patties warm or cold.
5. Enjoy.

STUFFED Bell Pepper Caps

🥣 Prep Time: 10 mins
⏱ Total Time: 40 mins

Servings per Recipe: 5
Calories   537.2
Fat   24.1g
Cholesterol   66.3mg
Sodium   597.7mg
Carbohydrates   55.1g
Protein   23.4g

Ingredients

- 5 large red bell peppers or 5 large green bell peppers
- 1 1/2 C. short grain brown rice, cooked
- 1 lb ground lamb
- 1/2 tsp salt
- 3 garlic cloves, minced
- 2 tbsp lemon juice
- 1/4 C. of fresh mint, finely chopped
- 1 tsp ground cinnamon
- 1 tsp ground cumin
- 1/4 tsp cayenne pepper
- 2 C. chicken broth

Directions

1. Remove the tops of the bell peppers and place them aside. Clean the peppers and discard the seeds.
2. Place the peppers in a pot and cover them with water. Cook them until the water start boiling.
3. Put on the lid and let them cook for 6 min over low medium heat. Remove the peppers from the water and place them aside to dry.
4. Place a large pan over medium heat cook in it the garlic with lamb for 8 min.
5. Turn off the heat then stir in the lemon juice, mint, spices, cooked rice and 3/4 C. of the broth.
6. Spoon the mix into the peppers and place their caps on top. Pour the remaining broth in a large saucepan.
7. Place in it the stuffed peppers. Cook them until the start boiling. Lower the heat and put on the lid.
8. Cook the stuffed peppers for 18 to 22 min. serve your stuffed peppers warm.
9. Enjoy.

Balsamic Carrots

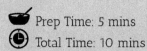

Prep Time: 5 mins
Total Time: 10 mins

Servings per Recipe: 2
Calories   163.5
Fat   13.7g
Cholesterol   0.0mg
Sodium   123.0mg
Carbohydrates   10.8g
Protein   0.7g

Ingredients
1 C. carrots, peeled and chopped or 1 C. baby carrots
2 tbsp olive oil or 2 tbsp clarified butter
1 tsp balsamic vinegar
1 pinch salt
1 pinch black pepper
1 tsp honey
1/4 lemon, juice of
1 pinch cinnamon

Directions
1. Place the carrots in a microwave safe bowl with 1 tbsp of water. Microwave it for 6 min.
2. Get a large shallow bowl: whisk in it the rest of the ingredients. Add the carrots and stir them well.
3. Serve your balsamic carrots.
4. Enjoy.

SAUCY
Seared Tuna

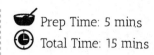
Prep Time: 5 mins
Total Time: 15 mins

Servings per Recipe: 4
Calories 363.2
Fat 21.0g
Cholesterol 79.9mg
Sodium 254.2mg
Carbohydrates 1.5g
Protein 40.0g

Ingredients

4 (6 oz) tuna steaks
1/2 tsp ground cumin
1 tsp paprika
1 tsp turmeric
1/4 tsp ground aniseed
1/2 tsp ground ginger
1/8-1/4 tsp ground cinnamon
1/4 tsp red pepper flakes

1/4 tsp salt
1/4 tsp pepper
1 tbsp fresh lemon juice
2 tbsp extra virgin olive oil, divided
2 tbsp butter, melted
4 tbsp ground fresh coriander

Directions

1. Get a small mixing bowl: mix in it the cumin, paprika, turmeric, anise, ginger, cinnamon, pepper flakes, salt, pepper, and lemon juice.
2. Brush the tuna steaks with 1 tbsp of olive oil then massage the spice mix into them.
3. Place a heavy large pan over medium high heat. Heat the remaining oil in it. Cook in it the tuna steaks for 1 to 2 min on each side.
4. Pour the melted butter all over the steaks then serve them right away.
5. Enjoy.

Algerian Pie of Chickpeas
(Garantita)

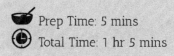

Prep Time: 5 mins
Total Time: 1 hr 5 mins

Servings per Recipe: 10
Calories   174.8
Total Fat   12.6g
Cholesterol   18.6mg
Sodium   719.3mg
Total Carbohydrate   10.7g
Protein   4.7g

Ingredients
2 C. chickpea flour
4 C. water
1/2 C. canola oil
1 tbsp salt
1/4 tsp black pepper
1 egg, beaten
ground cumin, for sprinkling
harissa, see appendix

Directions
1. Set your oven to 3750 degrees F before doing anything else.
2. In a food processor, add the flour, salt, oil and water and pulse till smooth.
3. Transfer the mixture into a 10x6-inch metal pan and top with beaten egg evenly.
4. Cook in the oven for about 1 hour.
5. Remove from oven and sprinkle with the cumin.
6. Cut the pie in desired slices and serve with harissa.

SWEET AND ZESTY
Chicken Stew

🥣 Prep Time: 15 mins
🕐 Total Time: 40 mins

Servings per Recipe: 8
Calories   312.3
Fat   7.2g
Cholesterol   76.8mg
Sodium   206.1mg
Carbohydrates   30.7g
Protein   30.5g

Ingredients

- 1/4 C. fresh lemon juice
- 2 tbsp honey
- 2 garlic cloves, crushed
- 1 tsp ground turmeric
- 1 tsp ground cumin
- 1 tsp ground cinnamon
- 1/4 tsp cayenne pepper
- 8 large skinless chicken breasts
- 8 wedges preserved lemons
- 1 1/2 C. chicken stock
- 1/3 C. slivered almonds
- 2 tsp olive oil
- 1 small yellow onion, halved, finely chopped
- 1 small red Chile, deseeded, finely chopped
- 1 C. couscous
- 1/3 C. currants
- 1/3 C. fresh coriander leaves, firmly packed

Directions

1. Get a casserole dish: mix in it the lemon juice, honey, garlic. Turmeric, cumin, cinnamon and cayenne pepper.
2. Place the chicken in the casserole and coat it with the mix. Cover it with a plastic wrap and place it in the fridge for 3 to 8 h.
3. Before you do anything preheat the oven to 360 F.
4. Drain the chicken from the marinade and reserve it. Place the chicken in a roasting pan and place the preserved lemon on it.
5. Place it in the oven to cook for 22 min.
6. Pour 1/2 C. of stock with the reserved marinade in a large pan. Cook them until they start boiling. Keeps it boiling for 6 min until it thickens?
7. Place a small skillet over medium heat. Toast in it the almonds for 3 min. place them aside.
8. Heat the oil in the same pan then cook in it the onion with chili for 3 min.
9. Stir in the rest of the stock then cook them until they start boiling.
10. Turn off the heat and combine in the couscous. Put on the lid and let it sit for 6 min.
11. Fluff the couscous with a fork then pour the thick marinade on it. Stir in the almonds and currants. Cook them for 3 min over low heat.
12. Turn off the heat then serve your couscous warm with the roasted chicken.
13. Enjoy.

Homemade Baklava (Algerian Style)

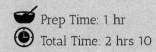

Prep Time: 1 hr
Total Time: 2 hrs 10

Servings per Recipe: 20
Calories   545.7
Total Fat   36.0g
Cholesterol   35.6mg
Sodium   231.2mg
Total Carbohydrate   51.3g
Protein   8.0g

Ingredients

24 oz. plain flour
310 ml water
200 ml melted ghee mixed with 110ml sunflower oil
1/2 tsp salt
18 oz. chopped almonds
128 g granulated sugar
1/4 tsp ground cinnamon
1 tsp vanilla sugar
2 tsps melted ghee
155 ml orange flower water (mazhar)

Glaze:
310 - 620 ml honey
155 - 310 ml orange flower water (mazhar)
310 ml extra of melted ghee, to brush the pastry

Directions

1. Set your oven to 300 degrees F before doing anything else and grease a large tray with a little melted ghee.
2. In a bowl, mix together the flour, salt and ghee/oil mixture.
3. Slowly, add the water and mix till a smooth dough forms.
4. Dust a smooth surface with the corn flour.
5. Divide the dough into 2 portions and place one onto floured surface, covered with a kitchen towel.
6. Shape another portion into golf sized balls.
7. Roll the balls into sausage shape and again roll onto floured surface into 3-4 mm thickness.
8. With a little corn flour, dust the dough sheets and process in the pasta machine on the lowest settings for thinnest strips.
9. Arrange the first strip vertically in the center of prepared tray and coat with ghee.

10. Place a second strip horizontally over the first strip.
11. Repeat with the remaining strips and ghee, covering the tray completely in 5 layers. (There should be 5 strips in each layer)
12. For filling in a food processor, add the almonds and pulse till chopped finely.
13. Transfer the almonds into a bowl with the sugar, vanilla sugar, cinnamon and mazhar and mix till well combined.
14. Place the filling over strips evenly in the tray and with a spatula, smooth the surface gently.
15. Roll the other dough portion and make golf size balls.
16. Roll the ball into sausage shape and again roll onto floured surface into 3-4 mm thickness.
17. With a little corn flour, dust the dough sheets and process in the pasta machine on the lowest settings for thinnest strips.
18. Place the strips over filling in the same process you have for the first portion. (This time you should have 6 layers of strips)
19. With a knife, cut the straight vertical lines all the way to bottom and then cut more lines diagonally to make diamond shape.
20. Press a whole almond in the center of each diamond.
21. Cook in the oven for about 60-70 minutes.
22. For syrup in a pan, warm the mazhar and honey.
23. Remove the baking treay from oven and pour the syrup over baklawa and keep aside for at least 10 minutes.
24. Cut into desired pieces and serve.

ALGERIAN
Ground Beef w/ Hominy

Prep Time: 15 mins
Total Time: 30 mins

Servings per Recipe: 6
Calories 217.0
Total Fat 8.2g
Cholesterol 49.1mg
Sodium 633.8mg
Total Carbohydrate 16.6g
Protein 18.4g

Ingredients
- 1 lb lean ground beef
- 1 1/2 C. onions, chopped
- 1 C. green bell pepper, chopped
- 3 garlic cloves, crushed
- 8 oz. canned kidney beans
- 8 oz. hominy
- 1 tsp salt
- 1 tsp dried basil
- 1/2 tsp ground black pepper
- 1/4 tsp sugar
- 1/4 tsp dried oregano
- 1/4 tsp red pepper flakes
- 2 C. water

Directions
1. In a large skillet, add the beef, bell pepper, onion and garlic on medium heat and cook for about 6 minutes.
2. Drain the excess fat and stir in the remaining ingredients and bring to a gentle boil.
3. Simmer for about 10 minutes till desired consistency.
4. This stew is great when served with pasta or rice.

FULL North African Couscous

Prep Time: 15 mins
Total Time: 1 hr 35 mins

Servings per Recipe: 4
Calories 361.6
Total Fat 2.5g
Cholesterol 0.0mg
Sodium 681.7mg
Total Carbohydrate 75.6g
Protein 13.3g

Ingredients
1 large onion, chopped
1/2 tsp turmeric
1/4 tsp cayenne
1/2 C. vegetable stock
1/2 tbsp cinnamon
1 1/2 tsps black pepper
1/2 tsp salt
5 tbsps tomato puree
3-4 whole cloves
3 medium zucchini
4 small yellow squash
3/4 large carrot
4 medium yellow potatoes, skins on
1 red bell pepper
1 (15 oz.) can garbanzo beans

Directions
1. In a large pan, heat the broth on medium-low heat and sauté the onion till soft.
2. Stir in the spices and sauté for a few minutes more.
3. Stir in the tomato paste and cook for about 2 minutes.
4. Meanwhile cut the the vegetables into large chunks.
5. In the pan, add all the vegetables, pinch of cinnamon and enough water that covers the mixture and bring to a boil.
6. Reduce the heat and simmer, covered for about for about 1-2 hours till desired doneness.
7. Stir in the beans and simmer for about 5 minutes.
8. Serve this veggie stew over the couscous.

Simple Kisra
(North African Flat Bread)

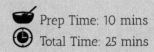

Prep Time: 10 mins
Total Time: 25 mins

Servings per Recipe: 8
Calories 209.9
Total Fat 7.1g
Cholesterol 0.0mg
Sodium 873.5mg
Total Carbohydrate 30.4g
Protein 5.2g

Ingredients
- 2 C. semolina flour
- 1 tbsp salt
- 1/4 C. olive oil
- 1 C. water

Directions
1. In a bowl, mix together all the ingredients except water.
2. Slowly, add the water and mix till a soft dough forms.
3. Make 2 equal sized balls from dough and flatten onto lightly floured surface to your desired size.
4. Heat a frying pan on medium heat and cook from both sides till golden brown.
5. Cut into desired size wedges before serving.

NORTH AFRICAN
Poached Eggs
(Chakchouka Algerian)

Prep Time: 15 mins
Total Time: 40 mins

Servings per Recipe: 4
Calories 252.8
Total Fat 15.5g
Cholesterol 186.0mg
Sodium 85.8mg
Total Carbohydrate 20.5g
Protein 9.4g

Ingredients

3 tbsps olive oil
1/2 tsp cumin seed
1 tbsp paprika
1 onion, thinly sliced
1 tbsp harissa
2 - 3 garlic cloves, minced
3 tomatoes, peeled, seeded and diced
1 potato, small diced cubes
1 green bell pepper, diced
1 red bell pepper, diced
1 yellow bell pepper, diced
1 - 2 chili pepper
1 C. water
kosher salt
fresh ground pepper
4 eggs
parsley or cilantro, chopped
black olives
capers

Directions

1. In a large deep skillet, heat the oil on medium heat and sauté cumin seeds for about 15 seconds.
2. Stir in the paprika and sauté for about 10 - 15 seconds.
3. Add the garlic and onion and sauté for about 5 minutes.
4. Stir in the tomatoes and bring to a simmer and stir in potatoes, peppers, water, salt and black pepper.
5. Reduce the heat to low and simmer, covered for at least 10 minutes.
6. Make 4 wells in the veggie mixture and carefully, crack 1 egg in each well.
7. Simmer, covered for about 10 minutes.
8. Serve with a garnishing of olives, capers and parsley.

Spicy Algerian Cucumbers
(Salatat Khiyar)

Prep Time: 15 mins
Total Time: 15 mins

Servings per Recipe: 2
Calories 301.6
Total Fat 30.7g
Cholesterol 0.0mg
Sodium 353.5mg
Total Carbohydrate 8.0g
Protein 1.5g

Ingredients

1 large cucumber, peeled, halved lengthwise, seeded, thinly sliced
1/2 green capsicum, cored, seeded and cut in half lengthwise
1/3 C. pitted and coarsely chopped green olives
4 large fresh mint leaves, finely chopped
2 tbsps finely chopped fresh coriander leaves
1/2 tsp paprika
1/4 C. extra virgin olive oil
3 1/2 tsps white wine vinegar
salt & freshly ground black pepper

Directions

1. In a large bowl, add all the ingredients and toss to coat well and serve immediately.

SWEET
Semolina Cake
(Basboussa)

Prep Time: 20 mins
Total Time: 50 mins

Servings per Recipe: 1
Calories   6699.1
Total Fat   290.2g
Cholesterol   775.8mg
Sodium   1180.8mg
Total Carbohydrate 963.8g
Protein   83.3g

Ingredients
Cake:
- 1 1/2 C. of coarse semolina
- 1 C. plain flour
- 2 tsps baking powder
- 3/4 C. unsweetened dried shredded coconut
- 1/4 C. granulated sugar
- 1 C. sunflower oil
- 1 lemon, zest of, finely grated
- 1 C. yogurt
- 4 eggs
- 2 tsps vanilla flavoring

Glaze:
- 3 C. water
- 3 C. granulated sugar
- 1 tbsp orange flower water
- 1 tsp lemon juice

Garnish:
- almonds

Directions
1. Set your oven to 355 degrees F before doing anything else and grease an 11x7-inch baking dish.
2. For Syrup in a pan, add the water and sugar and bring to a boil and simmer till pale golden syrup forms.
3. Remove from heat and immediately, stir in orange flower water and lemon juice and keep aside to cool.
4. In a large bowl ,mix together the flour, semolina, granulated sugar, baking powder and coconut.
5. In another bowl, add the remaining ingredients and beat till smooth and creamy.
6. Add the eggs mixture into flour mixture and mix till well combined.
7. Transfer the mixture into the prepared baking dish evenly and with the back of spatula, smooth the surface.
8. With a knife, make diamond pattern on top and insert 1 almond in each pattern.
9. Cook in the oven for about 30-40 minutes.
10. Remove the cake from oven and cut through the pattern.
11. Place the syrup over cake evenly and keep aside for about 2 hours.

Algerian Layered Cheese Pastry (Borek)

Prep Time: 1 hr
Total Time: 1 hr 5 mins

Servings per Recipe: 6
Calories   175.4
Total Fat   9.6g
Cholesterol   29.5mg
Sodium   128.8mg
Total Carbohydrate   12.6g
Protein   9.1g

Ingredients
250 g beef mince
1 onion, chopped
1 pinch cinnamon
1 1/2 C. parsley, finely chopped
2 eggs, beaten
6 phyllo pastry sheets
6 Laughing Cow cheese
vegetable oil

Directions
1. In a large skillet, heat a little oil and sauté the onion for about 5 minutes.
2. Stir in beef and cook till browned.
3. Stir in parsley, pinch of cinnamon, salt and black pepper.
4. Gently, stir in beaten eggs but take care not to scramble the eggs.
5. Remove from heat and let it cool.
6. Divide the beef mixture over each pastry sheet, about 1 1/2-inch from bottom and leaving about 1-inch from both sides.
7. Cut the cheese in half and place over the mixture.
8. Fold the both sides of pastry sheet to the middle and roll it.
9. Fry the rolls in a hot vegetable oil till golden brown.

TRADITIONAL
Butter Cookies
(Sables)

Prep Time: 25 mins
Total Time: 60 mins

Servings per Recipe: 1
Calories   142.4
Total Fat   3.9g
Cholesterol   7.4mg
Sodium   64.5mg
Total Carbohydrate   25.1g
Protein   1.6g

Ingredients
Cookies:
1 C. butter, softened
1/2 C. granulated sugar
1 large free range egg
2 1/2 C. all-purpose flour
1/2 tsp vanilla extract
Topping:
3/4 C. strawberry jam
1/2-3/4 C. icing sugar

Directions
1. Set your oven to 340 degrees F before doing anything else and line a baking tray with foil paper, shiny side up.
2. In a bowl, add the sugar and margarine and beat till fluffy.
3. Add the egg and vanilla extract and beat till well combined.
4. Slowly, add the flour and baking powder and mix till a soft dough forms.
5. On a floured surface with a rolling pin, roll the dough to 1/4-inch thickness.
6. Cut the tops and bottoms from dough and place onto prepared baking tray in a single layer.
7. Cook in the oven for about 8 minutes.
8. Remove from oven and keep aside to cool completely.
9. In a pan, add jam and heat till bubbling.
10. Remove from heat and let it cool slightly.
11. In a large tray, arrange the top of cookies and sprinkle with icing sugar.
12. Place about 1/2 tsp of jam over the underside of bottom of cookies.
13. Carefully, arrange the top cookies over jam.
14. Keep aside to set completely before serving.

North African Green Beans

Prep Time: 10 mins
Total Time: 15 mins

Servings per Recipe: 4
Calories 107.9
Total Fat 7.9g
Cholesterol 0.0mg
Sodium 7.8mg
Total Carbohydrate 8.8g
Protein 2.5g

Ingredients
- 1 lb fresh green beans
- 2 tbsps grapeseed oil
- 1 garlic clove, finely minced
- 1/2 tsp ground cumin
- 1/4 tsp paprika
- 1/4 tsp ground cloves
- 1 tbsp slivered almonds

Directions
1. Rinse and trim the green beans and cook in a pan of salted boiling water for about 1 minute.
2. Drain and rinse under cold water and transfer into a bowl.
3. In a skillet, heat oil on medium heat and sauté all the remaining ingredients for about 2 minutes.
4. Add the garlic mixture into the bowl with green beans and toss to coat well and serve warm.

SAUCY Algerian Carrots
(Zrodiya Mcharmla)

Prep Time: 10 mins
Total Time: 50 mins

Servings per Recipe: 4
Calories 148.2
Total Fat 10.6g
Cholesterol 0.0mg
Sodium 87.1mg
Total Carbohydrate 13.1g
Protein 1.4g

Ingredients
500 g carrots
3 tbsps olive oil
3 garlic cloves, minced
1 hot pepper
1/2 tsp caraway seed
1 tsp paprika
1 1/2 tbsps vinegar
salt and black pepper

Directions
1. Peel the carrots and then slice into rounds.
2. Cook the carrot in lightly salted water till tender enough.
3. Meanwhile for sauce in a grinder, add the garlic, caraway seeds, hot pepper and paprika and some salt and grind till a paste forms.
4. Transfer the sauce into a bowl and add the oil and 1 tbsp of water and mix till well combined.
5. Drain the carrots and return in the pan with sauce on low heat.
6. Cook, covered till the carrots absorb the flavor of sauce.
7. Stir in vinegar and serve hot.

Sweet Almond Cookies Pops
(Mchewek)

Prep Time: 15 mins
Total Time: 45 mins

Servings per Recipe: 1
Calories 95.1
Total Fat 5.9g
Cholesterol 15.6mg
Sodium 23.4mg
Total Carbohydrate 8.9g
Protein 2.8g

Ingredients
3 C. ground almonds
1 C. granulated sugar
3 small eggs
1 1/2 tsps baking powder
1/2 tsp vanilla extract
1/2 C. chopped almonds
glace cherries, to decorate

Directions
1. Set your oven to 340 degrees F before doing anything else and grease and flour a baking sheet.
2. In a large bowl, add ground almonds, sugar, vanilla and baking powder and mix till well combined.
3. Add eggs, one at a time and mix till a firm paste forms.
4. Make small equal sized ball from the mixture.
5. In a shallow dish, place chopped almonds.
6. Roll the balls into chopped almonds evenly and arrange onto prepared baking sheet in a single layer.
7. Gently, press 1/4 of a cherry in the center of each ball and cook in the oven for about 12 minutes.

FULL
Algerian Dinner
(Garbanzo Chicken Stew)

Prep Time: 15 mins
Total Time: 40 mins

Servings per Recipe: 6
Calories 230.8
Total Fat 5.1g
Cholesterol 35.0mg
Sodium 816.1mg
Total Carbohydrate 26.6g
Protein 19.9g

Ingredients
3 C. chicken broth
1 chicken bouillon cube
2 C. cooked chicken, chopped
1 medium onion, chopped
2 C. fresh green beans, cut
2 carrots, sliced
1 tsp ground cumin
1 tsp basil
1 garlic clove, minced
2 bay leaves
1/2 tsp dried parsley
salt
pepper
2 medium tomatoes, chopped
2 small zucchini, sliced
1 (16 oz.) can garbanzo beans, drained
1/4 tsp ground red pepper

Directions
1. In a large pan, add the chicken, carrots, green beans, onion, garlic, parsley, basil, cumin, bay leaves, salt, black pepper, bouillon cube and broth and bring to a boil.
2. Reduce the heat and simmer, covered for about 8 minutes.
3. Stir in the zucchini and tomatoes and cook for some time.
4. Stir in the beans and red pepper and cook till heated completely.
5. This stew will be great over a bowl of hot couscous.

Semolina Honey Dessert (Tamina)

Prep Time: 20 mins
Total Time: 30 mins

Servings per Recipe: 4
Calories   258.5
Total Fat   9.0g
Cholesterol   22.9mg
Sodium   2.0mg
Total Carbohydrate   39.0g
Protein   5.4g

Ingredients
- 1 C. of ground semolina
- 3 tbsps unsalted butter
- 2 tbsps of natural set honey

For The Decorations
- ground cinnamon
- silver dragees
- paper tea roses

Directions
1. In a pan, add the semolina on medium-high heat and cook, shaking the pan till toasted completely.
2. Transfer into a bowl and keep aside.
3. In the same pan, melt the butter and remove from heat and immediately stir the honey to combine well.
4. Place the semolina in the pan and stir to combine.
5. Transfer the Semolina mixture into a serving plate and sprinkle with cinnamon.
6. Serve with a garnishing of paper tea roses and silver dredges.

HOT
Carrots

🥣 Prep Time: 5 mins
🕐 Total Time: 20 mins

Servings per Recipe: 4
Calories   189.8
Total Fat   7.7g
Cholesterol   0.0mg
Sodium   505.7mg
Total Carbohydrate   30.2g
Protein   3.1g

Ingredients
2 1/2 lbs carrots, peeled and sliced
1/2 tsp hot sauce
2 tbsps light olive oil
3 garlic cloves, sliced thinly
1 lemon, juice of
2 tsps cumin seeds
1/2 tsp sugar
1/2 tsp salt
2 tbsps mint, finely chopped

Directions
1. In a steamer basket, steam the carrots for about 5 minutes.
2. Drain well, reserving about 5 tbsps of the cooking liquid.
3. Meanwhile heat a dry skillet and toast the cumin seeds till fragrant.
4. In a large pan, heat the oil and sauté the garlic for about 1 minute.
5. Stir in carrots, sugar, cumin seeds, salt, lemon juice, hot sauce and reserved cooking liquid on medium-low heat.
6. Cover partially and simmer for about 10 minutes.
7. Stir in mint and serve immediately.

Sesame Cookies
(Helouwa Ta'aba)

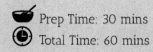

Prep Time: 30 mins
Total Time: 60 mins

Servings per Recipe: 1
Calories   105.1
Total Fat   4.1g
Cholesterol   18.6mg
Sodium   17.8mg
Total Carbohydrate   14.6g
Protein   2.2g

Ingredients
1 kg plain flour
6 eggs
250 g granulated sugar
2 tsps baking powder
1/4 liter sunflower oil
Lemon Version
4 lemons, zest of, finely grated

Directions
1. Line a cookie sheet with aluminum foil.
2. In a large bowl, add the oil and 6 eggs and beat well.
3. Add the lemon zest and baking powder and mix well.
4. Slowly, add the flour, beating continuously till a dough forms.
5. Place the dough onto a lightly floured surface and roll to 0.20-inch thickness.
6. With a cookie cutter, cut the desired size cookies and coat the top with the beaten egg.
7. Arrange the cookies onto prepared cookie sheet in a single layer.
8. Cook in the oven for about 25-28 minutes.

MINI
Almond Cakes
(Makrout a Louz)

Prep Time: 30 mins
Total Time: 50 mins

Servings per Recipe: 1
Calories 127.4
Total Fat 5.0g
Cholesterol 14.1mg
Sodium 5.7mg
Total Carbohydrate 19.2g
Protein 2.5g

Ingredients
Cake:
3 C. ground almonds
1 C. granulated sugar
4 limes, zest of, finely grated
3 small medium eggs
Prep:
3 tbsps cornflour
Garnish:
2 C. of light sugar syrup
2 1/2 C. icing sugar

Directions
1. Set your oven to 340 degrees F before doing anything else and arrange the rack in the middle shelf of the oven.
2. In a large bowl, add sugar, almonds, eggs and lime zest and mix till a soft dough forms.
3. Dust a smooth surface with corn flour.
4. Divide the dough into 4 portions and roll onto floured surface into a sausage shape.
5. Cut the each sausage into 1 1/4-inch diamond shape pieces.
6. Cook in the oven till set and pale in color.
7. Meanwhile for sugar syrup in a pan, cook 1 C. of sugar, 2 C. of water and half of a lime for about 10 minutes.
8. Remove from heat and cool slightly.
9. In a shallow dish, place icing sugar.
10. Remove the cookies from oven and let them cool slightly.
11. Dip the each diamond, one by one in the syrup and hold with a fork to discard excess syrup.
12. Then roll the diamond in icing sugar and keep aside.
13. After 5 minutes again roll into icing sugar.

North African Dinner Rolls

Prep Time: 1 hr 40 mins
Total Time: 2 hrs

Servings per Recipe: 1
Calories 88.7
Total Fat 2.4g
Cholesterol 14.1mg
Sodium 83.4mg
Total Carbohydrate 13.9g
Protein 2.8g

Ingredients
- 1/4 oz. active dry yeast
- 1/4 C. warm water, lightly salted
- 1 1/2 tbsps olive oil
- 1 C. farina (cream of wheat)
- 3/4 C. whole wheat flour
- 1/2 tsp salt
- 1/2 C. water
- 2 tbsps sesame seeds, toasted
- 1 egg, beaten
- cooking spray

Directions
1. In a bowl, mix together 1/4 C. of salted water and yeast and keep aside for at least 5 minutes.
2. In a large bowl, mix together farina, flour and salt and then add in olive oil.
3. Add the yeast mixture and stir to combine well.
4. Slowly, add 1/2 C. of water, stirring continuously till well a smooth dough forms.
5. With a damp cloth, cover the dough and keep in warm place for about 1 1/2 hours.
6. Set your oven to 400 degrees F and grease a baking sheet.
7. Just 2 minutes before baking, mix the sesame seeds in dough.
8. Divide the dough into 15 equal sized balls and arrange onto prepared baking sheet in a single layer.
9. Coat the each ball with the beaten egg and cook in the oven for about 20 minutes.

CHEESY Beef & Potato Casserole
(Batata Merhiya)

Prep Time: 30 mins
Total Time: 50 mins

Servings per Recipe: 6
Calories 241.6
Total Fat 14.8g
Cholesterol 77.3mg
Sodium 486.7mg
Total Carbohydrate 14.5g
Protein 12.4g

Ingredients
1 lb potato, peeled, boiled until tender
2 tbsps butter
1 tsp salt
2 tsps olive oil
1 small onion, finely chopped
1/2 lb ground beef
1/4 tsp pepper
1 medium egg, beaten
2 oz. gruyere cheese, grated

Directions
1. Set your oven to 350 degrees F before doing anything else and grease a casserole dish.
2. In a bowl, add the boiled potatoes, butter and salt and mash completely.
3. Heat a skillet and stir fry the beef, onion and pepper for about 5 minutes.
4. Drain the excess liquid and fat from the beef mixture.
5. Place the half of the potato mixture in the bottom of prepared casserole dish evenly.
6. Place the beef mixture and then topped with the remaining potato mixture evenly.
7. With the back of a spatula, smooth the surface of potato mixture.
8. Brush the top of the potato mixture with the beaten egg and sprinkle with the cheese evenly.
9. Cook in the oven for about 30 minutes.

Lemony Roasted Chicken
(Djedj Mechou)

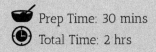 Prep Time: 30 mins
Total Time: 2 hrs

Servings per Recipe: 4
Calories 562.1
Total Fat 43.5g
Cholesterol 183.3mg
Sodium 2767.6mg
Total Carbohydrate 3.3g
Protein 38.1g

Ingredients
- 1 (3-4 lb) roasting chicken
- 2 lemons, halved
- 2 large garlic cloves, minced
- 3 tbsps unsalted butter
- 1 tbsp seasoning, mixed
- 1 1/2 tbsps coarse salt
- coarse salt
- fresh ground pepper
- olive oil
- 3-4 sprigs thyme

Directions
1. Set your oven to 450 degrees F before doing anything else and arrange a rack in a roasting pan.
2. In a mortar with pestle, mash the garlic with salt.
3. In a bowl, mix together the garlic paste, butter and spices.
4. With your fingers, loosen the skin under the breast and thighs.
5. With your fingers rub the butter mixture under the skin evenly and drizzle with the lemon juice.
6. Sprinkle the cavity and outer skin of the chicken with salt and black pepper.
7. Stuff the cavity of the chicken with thyme sprigs and 4 lemon halves.
8. Arrange the chicken into prepared roasting pan, breast side down.
9. Cook in the oven for about 15 minutes.
10. Remove the roasting pan from oven and place the chicken breast side up.
11. Now, reduce the temperature of oven to 350 degrees F.
12. Cook in the oven for about 90 minutes, basting with water and olive oil occasionally.
13. If chicken becomes brown too soon then cover with a foil paper for about 60-75 minutes and then remove before last 15 minutes of cooking.

SWEET & SOUR
Lamb with Pears

🥣 Prep Time: 10 mins
🕐 Total Time: 1 hr 10 mins

Servings per Recipe: 8
Calories　　　　　350.0
Total Fat　　　　　19.6g
Cholesterol　　　　86.4mg
Sodium　　　　　　96.6mg
Total Carbohydrate　23.4g
Protein　　　　　　21.0g

Ingredients
2 1/2 lbs lamb, cubed
3 tbsps butter
1/2 tsp ground cinnamon
3 C. water
1/4 C. sugar
16 prunes, soaked and drained
2 tbsps raisins
2 tbsps almonds
1 pear, peeled and cubed
1/4 C. orange juice

1 tsp orange blossom water (mazhar)

Directions
1. In a heavy-bottomed pan, melt the butter on low heat and stir fry the lamb for about 5 minutes.
2. Stir in the sugar, cinnamon and water and increase the heat to medium.
3. Simmer for about 40 minutes.
4. Stir in the remaining ingredients except the orange juice and simmer for about 15 minutes more.
5. Stir in the orange juice and serve immediately.

Algerian Date Appetizer

Prep Time: 15 mins
Total Time: 15 mins

Servings per Recipe: 1
Calories 20.8
Total Fat 0.0g
Cholesterol 0.0mg
Sodium 0.1mg
Total Carbohydrate 5.5g
Protein 0.1g

Ingredients

24 medjool dates
2 drops green food coloring
2/3 C. marzipan (almond paste)
2 tsps powdered sugar

Directions

1. Remove the pit of each date by cutting in the lengthwise.
2. In a bowl, add the almond paste and food coloring and stir to combine.
3. Stuff the dates with the almond paste mixture.
4. Serve with a sprinkling of the powdered sugar.

ALGERIAN
Saffron Soup

Prep Time: 10 mins
Total Time: 1 hr 10 mins

Servings per Recipe: 4
Calories   420.5
Total Fat   21.7g
Cholesterol   152.9mg
Sodium   715.0mg
Total Carbohydrate 6.3g
Protein   49.2g

Ingredients
- 2 tbsps olive oil
- 2 lbs boneless skinless chicken breasts, cubed
- 1 tbsp butter
- 4 garlic cloves, minced
- 1 tsp saffron, crumbled
- 1 bunch cilantro, finely chopped
- 1 C. water
- 8 oz. kalamata olives, pitted
- 1 lemon, juiced
- salt & freshly ground black pepper

Directions
1. In a large pan, heat the oil and stir fry the chicken for about 10 minutes.
2. Stir in the butter, saffron, cilantro and garlic and cook for about 10 minutes.
3. Stir in the water and bring to a boil and reduce the heat.
4. Simmer for about 25 minutes.
5. Stir in the lemon juice and olives and simmer for about 8 minutes more.
6. Season with the required amount of the salt and black pepper and remove from heat.
7. This stew will be great when served with rice or couscous.

Algerian Style Whole Chicken w/ Orzo

Prep Time: 15 mins
Total Time: 1 hr 45 mins

Servings per Recipe: 4
Calories   918.7
Total Fat   43.7g
Cholesterol   279.3mg
Sodium   473.8mg
Total Carbohydrate   73.5g
Protein   54.1g

Ingredients

- 1 whole chicken (or 6-8 pieces bone-in chicken)
- 3/4-1 C. canned chick-peas
- 2 tbsps ghee
- 1/4 tsp black pepper
- 1/2-3/4 tsp cinnamon
- 1 tsp tomato puree, concentrate
- 2 onions, chopped finely
- 1 -2 garlic clove, minced
- 1/2 tsp ras el hanout spice mix
- salt
- 3 -4 eggs
- 500 g orzo pasta
- 1 chicken stock cube
- olive oil

Directions

1. In a large pan, melt the ghee and stir fry the chicken, onions, ras el hanout, cinnamon and black pepper for about 10 minutes.
2. Stir in the chickpeas, tomato puree, chicken cube and required amount of water that covers the mixture and cook, covered on medium heat for about 90 minutes.
3. Meanwhile in a heatproof bowl, mix together pasta, 1/2 C. of water and a little bit of oil.
4. Arrange the bowl in the steamer and steam for about 15 minutes.
5. Remove from the steamer and use a little water to separate the pasta.
6. In a pan of the water, hard boil the eggs and then peel and half them.
7. In another large pan, add the pasta and gradually, add sauce from chicken mixture and cook till the pasta is done completely. (The mixture should be moist)
8. Transfer the pasta into the serving platter.
9. Top with the chicken pieces, followed by egg halves and remaining pan sauce.
10. Serve with the crusty bread and green salad.

ALGERIAN
Fava Beans

Prep Time: 10 mins
Total Time: 1 hr

Servings per Recipe: 4
Calories 277.7
Total Fat 10.8g
Cholesterol 0.0mg
Sodium 1140.1mg
Total Carbohydrate 33.1g
Protein 14.2g

Ingredients
1 kg broad bean, in the pod
1 bunch fresh cilantro, chopped
6 garlic cloves, minced
3-4 tbsps olive oil
1 tsp paprika
1/4 tsp cayenne
1/8 tsp black pepper
salt, to taste
1 -1 1/2 tsps vinegar
600 ml water

Directions
1. Trim the broad beans and remove the strings but leave the beans in their pod and then cut into 1-inch pieces.
2. In a heavy-bottomed pan, sauté the beans and garlic for about 2 minutes.
3. Stir in remaining ingredients and simmer, covered for about 25-30 minutes.
4. Simmer till desired thickness of sauce.

Sweet Algerian Harissa

Prep Time: 1 hr
Total Time: 1 hr

Servings per Recipe: 1
Calories   87.0
Total Fat   5.0g
Cholesterol   0.7mg
Sodium   2.7mg
Total Carbohydrate   9.6g
Protein   2.0g

Ingredients
4 C. ground almonds
1 1/4 C. sugar
1 tbsp butter
1/2 tsp orange blossom water (mazhar)
3 tbsps cornflour, for dusting
food coloring, of choice

For Decoration:
3 tbsps sugar, for rolling
glace cherries

Directions
1. In a food processor, add the sugar, almonds, butter and mazhar and pulse till a firm paste forms.
2. Divide the paste in 3 portions.
3. In a bowl, add 2 portions of the paste and food coloring and mix well.
4. Dust a smooth surface with the corn flour.
5. Roll the all three portions onto floured surface into sausage shape.
6. Cut the sausages into diamond shaped little pieces.
7. Press 1 cherry in the center of each diamond and serve in the tiny sweet cases.

ARTISANAL
Algerian Bread

🥣 Prep Time: 2 hrs
🕒 Total Time: 2 hrs 35 mins

Servings per Recipe: 1 loaf
Calories 18656.0
Total Fat 1800.5g
Cholesterol 554.9mg
Sodium 4767.1mg
Total Carbohydrate 562.0g
Protein 107.9g

Ingredients

3 1/2 C. fine semolina
1 1/4 C. strong white bread flour
2 C. water, room temp. plus extra
4 fluid oz. sunflower oil
7 g fast action yeast
1 large egg, beaten
2 tsps sugar
2 tsps salt
2 large egg yolks, beaten
2 - 3 tbsps sesame seeds

1 tbsp nigella seeds

Directions

1. Grease a large round metal pan.
2. In a larger bowl, mix together the flour, semolina, sugar, yeast and salt.
3. With your hand, make a well in the center.
4. Add the oil, egg and required amount of water and mix till a soft dough forms.
5. With your hands, knead the dough for about 30 minutes, adding more water occasionally if required.
6. Fold in the nigella seeds and with wet hands shape the dough into a ball.
7. Transfer the dough into prepared pan, pressing gently downwards.
8. Place some extra semolina on top evenly and keep aside, covered with the kitchen towel till rises to double in size.
9. Set your oven to 355 degrees F and arrange the rack in the upper 1/3 of the oven.
10. Coat the top of dough with the beaten egg yolks and top with sesame seeds evenly.
11. With a skewer, make 1 hole in the center of the dough and 5 about 1-inch from the edges.
12. Cook in the oven for about 35 minutes.
13. Remove from oven and let it cool for about 5 minutes before removing from the pan.

Algerian Egg Rolls

🥣 Prep Time: 25 mins
🕐 Total Time: 1 hr

Servings per Recipe: 10
Calories   68.5
Total Fat   2.2g
Cholesterol   5.6mg
Sodium   158.4mg
Total Carbohydrate   9.6g
Protein   2.3g

Ingredients

20 - 24 spring rolls, pastry sheets
2 1/2 - 3 C. mashed potatoes
3/4 - 1 C. cheddar cheese, grated
1/2 medium brown onion, finely chopped
1 medium pickled gherkin, finely chopped
3 tbsps fresh parsley, finely chopped
1 tbsp butter
salt
black pepper
flour, & water for the paste

Directions

1. For filling in a large bowl, mix together all the ingredients except spring roll sheets.
2. Arrange the spring rolls onto a smooth surface.
3. Divide the filling between pastry rolls evenly, by placing in the center, leaving 1-inch space from all sides.
4. Place the left side over filling and then repeat with the right one.
5. Now, place the bottom over filling to cover it.
6. With a pastry brush, coat the edges with the flour paste.
7. Fold the rolls to secure the filling and fry the rolls in little oil till golden brown from all sides.

NORTH AFRICAN
Breakfast Quiche

Prep Time: 5 mins
Total Time: 35 mins

Servings per Recipe: 4
Calories 235.1
Total Fat 7.2g
Cholesterol 279.0mg
Sodium 489.2mg
Total Carbohydrate 29.3g
Protein 11.1g

Ingredients
6 eggs
1/2 tsp salt
4 -5 tsps vanilla flavoring
5 tbsps self raising flour
2 tbsps fine semolina
1 tsp baking powder
To serve
1/4-1/2 C. honey

Directions
1. In a large blender, add all the ingredients and pulse till a thick and bubbly mixture forms.
2. Heat a greased skillet on low heat and add the mixture evenly.
3. Cook for about 15 minutes and carefully change the side and cook for about 15 minutes more.
4. Meanwhile warm the honey till melted slightly.
5. Transfer the pancake into a serving platter and cut into equal sized 8 wedges.
6. Serve warm with a drizzling of the honey.

Algerian Stuffed Grape Leaves
(Dolmas Dalya)

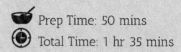

Prep Time: 50 mins
Total Time: 1 hr 35 mins

Servings per Recipe: 1 casserole
Calories   30.0
Total Fat   0.5g
Cholesterol   0.0mg
Sodium   138.5mg
Total Carbohydrate 5.7g
Protein   0.7g

Ingredients

Dolmas:
50 grape leaves
1 large red pepper, chopped finely
1 large red vine-ripened tomatoes, chopped finely
1/2 large onion, chopped finely
4 garlic cloves, minced
1 1/2 C. basmati rice
1 tsp paprika
1/2 tsp cinnamon
1/2 tsp ras el hanout spice mix
1 tbsp olive oil
4 tbsps water
salt and black pepper

Topping:
1/2 large onion
1 large vine-ripened tomatoes
2 garlic cloves, minced
1/2 tsp cinnamon
1 chicken stock cube
1 liter water
1 tsp lemon juice
salt and black pepper

Directions

1. For the preparation of fresh vine leaves, wash them and then trim the stalks.
2. In a lightly salted boiling water, blanch the leaves for about 15 minutes.
3. Rinse the leaves then drain well and keep aside.
4. For filling in a large skillet, heat a little oil and stir fry the pepper, onion, tomatoes and garlic for about 4 minutes.
5. Stir in the all spices and cook for about 30 seconds.
6. Remove from heat and immediately, stir in rice, water and olive oil and keep aside.
7. Arrange the leaves onto a smooth surface.
8. Pace about the 1 tsp of the filling mixture in the bottom center of each leaf.
9. First, fold the left corner over filling and then the right one.
10. Gently roll the leaf to secure the filling.

11. In a larger pan, place the rolls in 2-3 layers.
12. Place a large heatproof plate over the rolls.
13. In a bowl, mix together all sauce ingredients and then place over rolls evenly.
14. Cook, covered on medium heat for about 25 minutes.
15. Serve these rolls with a drizzling of lemon juice.

Simply Roasted Chicken

🥣 Prep Time: 5 mins
🕐 Total Time: 1 hr 35 mins

Servings per Recipe: 4
Calories 305.9
Total Fat 23.1g
Cholesterol 100.3mg
Sodium 132.1mg
Total Carbohydrate 2.5g
Protein 21.6g

Ingredients
- 1 chicken
- 1 lemon
- 2 garlic cloves, crushed
- 1 bunch thyme
- 2 tbsps butter
- 1/2 tbsp ground cumin
- 1/2 tbsp ground coriander

Directions
1. Set your oven to 392 degrees F before doing anything else.
2. In a bowl, mix together the garlic, butter, spices and salt.
3. With your fingers, loosen the skin under the breast and thighs.
4. With your fingers rub the butter mixture under the skin and over the skin evenly and drizzle with the lemon juice.
5. Stuff the cavity of the chicken with thyme bunch and lemon halves.
6. Sprinkle the chicken with the salt and black pepper generously.
7. Arrange the chicken into prepared roasting pan, breast side down.
8. Cook in the oven for about 80-90 minutes.

ALGERIAN
Tomato Salad

Prep Time: 10 mins
Total Time: 50 mins

Servings per Recipe: 2
Calories 93.4
Total Fat 2.9g
Cholesterol 0.0mg
Sodium 14.1mg
Total Carbohydrate 16.7g
Protein 3.2g

Ingredients
3 large green bell peppers
2 vine ripened tomatoes
1 - 2 garlic clove, minced
2 - 3 tbsps water
1 tsp olive oil
salt
vinegar, to taste

Directions
1. Grill the peppers till softened and immediately place in a zip lock bag and keep aside for at least 5 minutes.
2. Carefully peel the peppers and chop into 1 1/2-inch pieces.
3. In a skillet, heat oil on medium heat and sauté the tomatoes, peppers and garlic for a few minutes.
4. Stir in salt, black pepper and water and cook, stirring occasionally for about 15 minutes.
5. Serve with a drizzling of vinegar alongside crusty bread.

North African Meatballs

Prep Time: 15 mins
Total Time: 45 mins

Servings per Recipe: 8
Calories   120.8
Total Fat   3.0g
Cholesterol   59.4mg
Sodium   279.2mg
Total Carbohydrate 7.9g
Protein   14.7g

Ingredients
- 1 lb chopped beef
- 1/2 C. breadcrumbs
- 1 tbsp chopped fresh parsley
- 1 dash nutmeg
- 1/2 tsp onion powder
- salt and pepper
- 1 egg, slightly beaten
- Sauce
- 1/2 C. chopped onion
- 2 tomatoes, chopped
- 1 tbsp chopped fresh parsley
- 1/2 tsp salt
- 1 dash saffron
- 1 dash cinnamon
- 1 dash pepper
- 1/2 C. tomato juice

Directions
1. In a large bowl, add the beef, egg, breadcrumbs, parsley, onion powder, nutmeg, salt, black pepper and water and mix till well combined.
2. Make equal sized balls from the mixture and cook under broiler till golden brown.
3. In a steamer, steam the onion and tomatoes.
4. In a pan, add the meatballs, steamed veggies, tomato juice and remaining spices and simmer, covered for about 30 minutes.

A DELICIOUS
Stew in Tunisia

Prep Time: 10 mins
Total Time: 40 mins

Servings per Recipe: 4
Calories 235.0
Total Fat 2.0g
Cholesterol 0.0mg
Sodium 401.0mg
Total Carbohydrate 49.1g
Protein 9.1g

Ingredients

1 thinly sliced onion
1/4 C. vegetable broth
3 C. thinly sliced cabbage
1 dash salt
1 large green pepper, diced
1 (28 oz.) can diced tomatoes, undrained
1 (16 oz.) can chickpeas
1/4 C. raisins
2 tsps ground coriander
1/2 tsp turmeric
1/4 tsp cinnamon
1 tbsp lemon juice
salt

Directions

1. In a pan, heat the broth and sauté the onion for about 5 minutes.
2. Stir in the cabbage and salt and sauté for about 5 minutes.
3. Stir in the green pepper and spices and sauté for about 1 minutes.
4. Stir in the chickpeas, tomatoes and raisins and simmer, covered for about 15 minutes.
5. Serve with a drizzling of the lemon juice alongside couscous.

Hot Harissa Chicken

🥣 Prep Time: 5 mins
🕐 Total Time: 55 mins

Servings per Recipe: 4
Calories 219.0
Total Fat 4.0g
Cholesterol 7.2mg
Sodium 664.6mg
Total Carbohydrate 34.2g
Protein 11.5g

Ingredients

- 8 chicken legs
- 1 small onion, chopped finely
- 4 garlic cloves, crushed
- 1/2 tsp ras el hanout spice mix, see appendix
- 1/4 tsp harissa, see appendix
- 2 allspice berries
- 2 tsps tomato paste
- 400 g chickpeas, drained
- 2 pints chicken stock

Directions

1. In a large pan, heat the 2 tbsps of oil and sauté the onion till tender.
2. Stir in the chicken and stir fry for about 10 minutes.
3. Stir in the tomato puree, garlic, harissa, spices and salt and cook for about 2 minutes.
4. Stir in the broth and bring to a boil and simmer for about 30 minutes.
5. Stir in the chickpeas and simmer for about 10 minutes.

TUNISIAN Squash

Prep Time: 10 mins
Total Time: 30 mins

Servings per Recipe: 4
Calories   93.6
Total Fat   7.2g
Cholesterol   0.0mg
Sodium   301.4mg
Total Carbohydrate   6.8g
Protein   1.7g

Ingredients

- 2 crookneck yellow squash, cut in cubes
- 2 zucchini, cut in cubes
- 1 onion, diced
- 2 tbsp olive oil
- 1 tsp paprika
- 1/2 tsp cumin
- 1/2 tsp pepper
- 1/2 tsp salt
- 1/4 tsp caraway seed, ground
- 1/4 tsp red pepper flakes
- 2 garlic cloves, crushed
- 1/4 C. water

Directions

1. In a skillet, heat the oil and sauté the onion and garlic till soft.
2. Stir in the spices and sauté for a while.
3. Stir in the squash and water and simmer on low heat till done completely.

North African Chicken Soup

Prep Time: 5 mins
Total Time: 2 hrs 15 mins

Servings per Recipe: 6
Calories   160.5
Total Fat   6.9g
Cholesterol   70.1mg
Sodium   156.4mg
Total Carbohydrate 12.1g
Protein   12.0g

Ingredients

- 4 chicken drumsticks, skinless
- 1 medium brown onion, finely diced
- 200 g canned chick-peas, rinsed & drained
- 2 1/2 liters water
- 2 inches cinnamon sticks
- 1/2 lemon, juice of
- 1 large egg yolk, beaten
- 1/4 C. fresh parsley, finely chopped
- 2 - 3 tsps olive oil
- 1 1/2 tbsps basmati rice
- salt & pepper

Directions

1. In a large pan, heat the oil and sauté the onion till soft.
2. Stir in the chicken and cinnamon sticks and stir fry for about 8 minutes.
3. Stir in the salt, black pepper and water and bring to a boil.
4. Reduce the heat to medium and simmer, covered for about 75 minutes.
5. Remove the chicken from the pan and let it cool slightly.
6. Remove the chicken from bones and add in the pan with the chickpeas.
7. Simmer, covered for about 15 minutes.
8. Stir in the rice and seasoning if required and simmer, covered for about 15 minutes.
9. In a bowl, add the egg yolk, lemon juice and a few tsps of the broth and beat well.
10. Slowly, add the egg yolk mixture, stirring continuously and simmer for about 1 minute.
11. Stir in the parsley and serve hot.

TUNISIAN
Lamb Quiche

Prep Time: 20 mins
Total Time: 1 hr 5 mins

Servings per Recipe: 6
Calories 382.7
Total Fat 27.5g
Cholesterol 242.6mg
Sodium 273.2mg
Total Carbohydrate 12.2g
Protein 20.2g

Ingredients
1 large onion, chopped
1 lb lean ground lamb
2 tbsp vegetable oil
1 1/2 C. mashed potatoes
2 hard-cooked eggs, chopped
2 tbsp parsley, chopped
salt and pepper
1/2 tsp garlic powder
4 eggs, lightly beaten

Directions
1. Set your oven to 375 degrees F before doing anything else and lightly grease a 9-inch round baking pan.
2. In a large bowl, add all the ingredients and mix till well combined.
3. Transfer the mixture into prepared baking pan evenly.
4. Cook in the oven for about 45 minutes.
5. Remove from oven and let it cool slightly.
6. Cut into desired size wedges and serve.

Pasta Tunisian

Prep Time: 10 mins
Total Time: 30 mins

Servings per Recipe: 4
Calories   700.0
Total Fat   32.3g
Cholesterol   63.0mg
Sodium   813.3mg
Total Carbohydrate   81.4g
Protein   22.4g

Ingredients
- 375 g penne pasta
- 2 onions, minced
- 2 tbsp olive oil
- 350 g merguez sausages, cut in diagonal sections of 1 inch
- 2 tbsp tomato paste
- 1 C. chicken broth
- 3 tbsp fresh parsley, chopped
- salt and pepper

Directions
1. In a pan of lightly salted boiling water, cook the pasta till desired doneness.
2. Drain well and coat with a little oil and keep aside.
3. In a large skillet, heat the oil and sauté onion till golden brown.
4. Stir in the sausage, salt and black pepper and cook till golden brown from both sides.
5. Stir in the tomato paste and cook for about 1 minute.
6. Stir in the broth and bring to a gentle boil.
7. Simmer slowly till the sausages are done completely.
8. Stir in the pasta and cook till heated completely.
9. Stir in the seasoning and parsley and serve.

TUNISIAN Poached Eggs
(Shakshouka)

Prep Time: 10 mins
Total Time: 40 mins

Servings per Recipe: 4
Calories 168.2
Total Fat 8.9g
Cholesterol 186.0mg
Sodium 375.7mg
Total Carbohydrate 14.5g
Protein 8.9g

Ingredients

1 tbsp extra virgin olive oil
1 tsp cumin seed
1 tbsp paprika
1 onion, thinly sliced
2 garlic cloves, minced
3 tomatoes, peeled, seeded and diced
2 green bell peppers, sliced
2 red bell peppers, sliced
1 tbsp harissa
1 C. water
sea salt, to taste
black pepper
4 eggs, large
parsley, finely chopped for garnish

Directions

1. In a deep skillet, heat the oil on medium heat and sauté the paprika and cumin seeds for about 10-15 seconds.
2. Stir in the onion and garlic and sauté for about 5 minutes.
3. Stir in the tomatoes and cook for about 3-4 minutes.
4. Stir in harissa, bell peppers, salt, black pepper and the water and bring to a boil.
5. Reduce the heat to low and simmer, covered for about 10 minutes.
6. With a spoon, make 4 wells in the veggie mixture and carefully crack 1 egg in each well.
7. Cover the pan and cook for about 10 minutes.
8. Serve with a garnishing of parsley alongside the crusty bread.

Tunisia Breakfast Eggs

Prep Time: 35 mins
Total Time: 50 mins

Servings per Recipe: 4
Calories   186.6
Total Fat   12.1g
Cholesterol   211.5mg
Sodium   78.4mg
Total Carbohydrate 12.6g
Protein   8.3g

Ingredients
2 tbsp olive oil
1 onion, thinly sliced
1 red bell pepper, cut into strips
1 yellow bell pepper, cut into strips
1 fresh red chili pepper, seeded and finely chopped
6 plum tomatoes, peeled, seeded and quartered
salt & freshly ground black pepper
2 tsps chopped of fresh mint
4 eggs

Directions
1. In a large heavy-bottomed skillet, heat the oil and sauté the onion for about 5 minutes.
2. Stir in the chili pepper and bell peppers and cook, covered for about 8 minutes.
3. Stir in the tomatoes and cook, covered for about 5-8 minutes.
4. With a spatula, make 4 wells in the peppers mixture and reduce the heat to low.
5. Carefully crack 1 egg in each well and cook, covered for about 5 minutes, basting the eggs with the pan juices occasionally.
6. Serve with a garnishing of the mint sprig.

FULL
Tunisian Breakfast
(Spicy Sausage Omelet)

Prep Time: 10 mins
Total Time: 20 mins

Servings per Recipe: 2
Calories 403.2
Total Fat 31.5g
Cholesterol 412.8mg
Sodium 506.1mg
Total Carbohydrate 7.1g
Protein 22.1g

Ingredients
4 eggs
1/4 lb ground sausage
1/2 C. onion, diced
1 garlic clove, minced
1/4 tsp caraway seed, ground
1/2 tsp paprika
1 tbsp olive oil
1/8 cayenne
1/2 C. green pepper, diced

Directions
1. In a skillet, heat the oil and sauté the onion, peppers and sausage.
2. Stir in the garlic and spices and sauté a little.
3. Lightly, grease a frying pan and heat it.
4. Add the beaten eggs evenly and cook till set.
5. Place the filling over half side and cover with other half.
6. Transfer into the plate and serve.

Tunisian Chicken Cutlets

Prep Time: 10 mins
Total Time: 1 hr 25 mins

Servings per Recipe: 8
Calories   326.0
Total Fat   18.7g
Cholesterol   92.8mg
Sodium   431.8mg
Total Carbohydrate 7.6g
Protein   31.3g

Ingredients

- 4 whole chicken breasts, split
- 3 tbsp all-purpose flour
- 1 tsp salt
- 1/4 tsp pepper
- 3 tbsp vegetable oil
- 1 1/2 C. onions, chopped
- 2 garlic cloves, minced
- 1/2 tsp paprika
- 1/2 tsp cumin
- 1 pinch cayenne pepper
- 1/2 C. chicken broth
- 1 lemon, juice of, small
- 1 small lemon, thinly sliced
- pimiento, stuffed green olives, halved
- 1 tbsp chopped fresh parsley

Directions

1. Set your oven to 375 degrees F before doing anything else.
2. In a large bowl, mix together the flour, salt and black pepper.
3. Add the chicken and coat with flour mixture evenly and the shake off the excess.
4. In a large skillet, heat the oil and stir fry the chicken in batches till golden brown.
5. Transfer the mixture into a 13x9-inch baking dish in a single layer.
6. In the same skillet, sauté the onion, garlic and spices till onions become soft.
7. Stir in the lemon juice and broth and bring to a boil, scraping the brown bits.
8. Place the broth mixture over chicken evenly, followed by lemon slices.
9. Cook, covered in the oven for about 40 minutes.
10. Uncover the baking dish and top with olives evenly and cook for about 5 minutes more.
11. Serve with a garnishing of the parsley.

TUNISIAN
Lunch Box
(Cucumber Apple Salad)

Prep Time: 10 mins
Total Time: 20 mins

Servings per Recipe: 4
Calories   220.7
Total Fat   14.1g
Cholesterol   0.0mg
Sodium   591.0mg
Total Carbohydrate   25.9g
Protein   2.5g

Ingredients
2 granny smith apples
2 cucumbers
2 tomatoes
1 bell pepper
1/2 purple onion
Dressing
2 lemons, juice of
1/8 C. tarragon vinegar
1/4 C. olive oil, scant
1 tsp salt

1 - 2 tbsp mint, finely ground

Directions
1. Peel, core and chop the apples and then chop the vegetables finely.
2. In a large bowl, mix together the apples and vegetables.
3. In another bowl, add all the dressing ingredients and mix till well combined.
4. Pour the dressing over salad and mix well.
5. Keep aside for about 2 hours before serving.

Orange Chicken

Prep Time: 10 mins
Total Time: 50 mins

Servings per Recipe: 4
Calories 216.3
Total Fat 4.1g
Cholesterol 75.5mg
Sodium 378.2mg
Total Carbohydrate 15.6g
Protein 28.7g

Ingredients
- 1 red onion, finely sliced
- 4 boneless skinless chicken breasts, cut into strips
- 2 garlic cloves, chopped
- 1 tsp coriander seed
- 1 tsp ground cumin
- 1 tsp ground cinnamon
- 1/2 tsp cayenne pepper
- 6 cardamom pods, crushed with seeds removed
- 1 1/4 C. chicken broth
- 2 tbsp all-purpose flour
- 1 tsp dried oregano
- 1 (14 oz.) can chopped tomatoes
- 2 pieces orange peel
- 2/3 C. orange juice
- salt & freshly ground black pepper

Directions
1. Heat a large nonstick frying pan and sauté the onion for about 2-3 minutes.
2. Stir in the chicken and garlic and stir fry till golden brown from all the sides.
3. Stir in the 2-3 tbsp of the broth, flour and spices and cook, stirring for about 1 minute.
4. Slowly, add the broth, stirring continuously and stir in tomatoes, oregano and orange peel.
5. Simmer, covered for about 20 minutes.
6. Stir in the seasoning and serve.

HARISSA
Tunisian Style

🥣 Prep Time: 25 mins
🕐 Total Time: 45 mins

Servings per Recipe: 1 jar
Calories 1115.6
Total Fat 111.4g
Cholesterol 0.0mg
Sodium 1200.5mg
Total Carbohydrate 32.2g
Protein 7.2g

Ingredients
4 smoked chili peppers, such as ancho or chipotle
8 dried New Mexico hot red chili pepper
1 tbsp cumin seed
2 tsps coriander seeds
1 tsp caraway seed
8 garlic cloves
1/2 C. olive oil
1/2 tsp salt

Directions
1. Discard the stems and seeds of the chiles and place in a large bowl of the boiling water for about 20 minutes.
2. Heat a nonstick frying pan on medium-high heat and toast the caraway seeds, coriander and cumin for about 2-3 minutes.
3. Remove from heat and keep aside to cool completely.
4. In a blender, place the toasted seeds and pulse till powdered.
5. Add the remaining ingredients and pulse till a smooth paste forms.
6. Transfer the paste into an airtight container and refrigerate to preserve for up to 2 months.

Lemony Chickpeas Soup
(Leblabi)

Prep Time: 10 mins
Total Time: 40 mins

Servings per Recipe: 8
Calories 155.4
Total Fat 4.5g
Cholesterol 0.0mg
Sodium 298.7mg
Total Carbohydrate 24.3g
Protein 5.1g

Ingredients
- 2 tbsp olive oil
- 5 cloves garlic, minced
- 2 jalapeno peppers, minced
- 1 tsp ground caraway
- 1 tsp dried oregano
- 2 (14 oz.) cans chickpeas, drained and rinsed
- 2 (14 oz.) cans vegetable broth
- 2 C. water
- 5 tbsp fresh lemon juice
- 1/3 C. fresh cilantro, chopped
- salt and pepper

Directions
1. In a large soup pan, heat the oil on medium heat and sauté the jalapeños and garlic till golden brown.
2. Stir in the oregano and caraway seeds and sauté for a couple minutes.
3. Stir in the chickpeas, water and broth and simmer for about 20 minutes.
4. Stir in the seasoning, cilantro and lemon juice and simmer for about 5 minutes.

LAMB
Tagine Tunisian

Prep Time: 30 mins
Total Time: 1 hr 15 mins

Servings per Recipe: 4
Calories   538.1
Total Fat   36.1g
Cholesterol   469.3mg
Sodium   834.4mg
Total Carbohydrate   20.5g
Protein   36.8g

Ingredients

Meat:
2 tbsp olive oil
2 medium onions, finely chopped
1/2 lb ground lamb
4 garlic cloves, crushed
1 tbsp ground coriander
salt and pepper, to taste
chili powder, to taste
Lower layer (1/3 of meat base and)
2 lbs spinach (blanches, squeezed and chopped)
3 eggs, lightly beaten
Middle layer (1/3 of meat base and)
3 - 4 oz. gruyere, cheese
6 oz. fresh ricotta cheese
3 eggs, lightly beaten
Upper layer (1/3 of meat base and)
1 C. parsley, fresh, chopped
3 eggs, lightly beaten

Directions

1. Set your oven to 350 degrees F before doing anything else and grease a 10-15-inch baking mold with 1 tbsp of the olive oil and place in the oven.
2. For meat base in a skillet, heat the remaining oil and sauté the onion till tender.
3. Stir in lamb and cook till done completely.
4. Remove from heat and immediately, stir in the remaining ingredients.
5. Divide the lamb mixture in 3 portions.
6. For lower layer in a bowl, mix together the all ingredients and the first portion of the meat mixture.
7. Remove the heated mold from oven.
8. Place the lower layer mixture in heated mold evenly and with the back of a spoon, smooth the surface.
9. Cook in the oven for about 10 minutes.
10. Meanwhile for middle layer in a bowl, mix together all the ingredients and the second portion of meat mixture.
11. Remove the mold from oven and place the second layer mixture over the first layer.
12. With the back of a spoon, smooth the surface and cook in the oven for about 10 minutes.
13. Meanwhile for upper layer in a bowl, mix together all the ingredients and the third portion of the meat mixture.

14. Remove the mold from oven and place the upper layer mixture over middle layer.
15. With the back of a spoon, smooth the surface and cook in the oven for about 10-15 minutes more.
16. Remove from the oven and keep aside for about 20 minutes before slicing.

TABIL
North African Spice Mix

🥣 Prep Time: 10 mins
🕐 Total Time: 10 mins

Servings per Recipe: 1 bottle
Calories 416.3
Total Fat 20.7g
Cholesterol 0.0mg
Sodium 41.7mg
Total Carbohydrate 75.0g
Protein 18.7g

Ingredients
2 large garlic cloves, peeled, chopped and dried in the open air for 2 days
1/4 C. coriander seed
1 tbsp caraway seed
2 tsps cayenne pepper

Directions
1. In a mortar with the pestle, grind the galic, caraway, corinder and cayenne till smooth.
2. Preserve in the refrigerator.

North African Zucchini

Prep Time: 10 mins
Total Time: 20 mins

Servings per Recipe: 4
Calories 144.4
Total Fat 13.7g
Cholesterol 0.0mg
Sodium 12.1mg
Total Carbohydrate 5.5g
Protein 1.6g

Ingredients

1 lb zucchini, sliced
4 tbsp olive oil
3 tbsp lemon juice
2 garlic cloves, crushed
1 tsp caraway seed, crushed
1 pinch paprika
salt and pepper, to your taste

Directions

1. In a steamer, steam the zucchini till done and drain well.
2. Transfer the zucchini into a bowl.
3. In another bowl, add the remaining ingredients except the paprika and mix well.
4. Pour dressing over zucchini and mix well.
5. Serve with a sprinkling of the paprika.

SWEET
Parsnips

🥣 Prep Time: 10 mins
🕐 Total Time: 28 mins

Servings per Recipe: 4
Calories 182.8
Total Fat 10.5g
Cholesterol 0.0mg
Sodium 13.8mg
Total Carbohydrate 22.3g
Protein 1.4g

Ingredients
1 lb parsnip, peeled sliced longways
1 C. water
3 tbsp olive oil
1 garlic clove, crushed
1/4 tsp red pepper flakes
1/4 tsp caraway seed, ground
1/4 tsp cumin
1/4 tsp coriander seed, ground
1 tsp honey
1/4 C. vegetable broth

Directions
1. In a pan of water, cook the parsnips for about 8 minutes and drain well.
2. In a skillet, heat the oil and sauté the onion and garlic till tender.
3. Stir in the spices and sauté for a while.
4. Stir in the parsnips, honey and broth abd cook for about 10 minutes.

Tunisian Egg Scramble

🥣 Prep Time: 15 mins
🕐 Total Time: 30 mins

Servings per Recipe: 3
Calories   464.1
Total Fat   10.8g
Cholesterol   423.0mg
Sodium   170.0mg
Total Carbohydrate   71.5g
Protein   21.3g

Ingredients

- 2 green peppers, cleaned and cut into strips
- 2 medium onions, sliced
- 4 roma tomatoes, sliced into 1/3s
- 5 red potatoes, washed, unpeeled and sliced
- olive oil
- salt and pepper
- cayenne pepper
- 6 eggs

Directions

1. In a skillet, heat the oil on low heat and cook the onion, peppers, potatoes and spices till tender.
2. Stir in the tomatoes and increase the heat to medium.
3. In a bowl, beat the eggs and place in the skillet.
4. Cook, stirring continuously till the desired doneness of scramble.

TUNISIAN COUSCOUS

Prep Time: 15 mins
Total Time: 30 mins

Servings per Recipe: 6
Calories   370.2
Total Fat   3.9g
Cholesterol   0.0mg
Sodium   345.0mg
Total Carbohydrate   70.9g
Protein   13.0g

Ingredients

- 1 tbsp olive oil
- 1 red onion, chopped
- 1 zucchini, coarsely chopped
- 1 yellow squash, coarsely chopped
- 1 carrot, coarsely chopped
- 1 red bell pepper, coarsely chopped
- 1 yellow bell pepper, coarsely chopped
- 1/2 C. sliced baby portabella mushrooms
- 4 C. vegetable broth
- 1/2 tsp smoked sweet paprika
- 1/4 tsp ground cardamom
- 1/4 tsp salt
- 1 tbsp chopped fresh cilantro
- 1 (16 oz.) can chickpeas, drained
- 2 roma tomatoes, sliced
- 2 C. dry couscous
- 1 tsp grated orange zest
- 1 tbsp grated parmesan cheese
- 1/2 tsp paprika
- 1 tbsp finely chopped toasted almond

Directions

1. In a large pan, heat the oil on medium-low heat and cook the onion, carrot, squash and zucchini for about 5 minutes, stirring occasionally.
2. Stir in the mushrooms and bell peppers and cook or about 2-3 minutes.
3. Stir in the cilantro, spices and broth and bring to a boil.
4. Reduce the heat to low and stir in the chickpeas, couscous and tomatoes.
5. Cover the pan and immediately remove from the heat and keep aside for about 5 minutes.
6. With a fork, fluff the mixture slightly.
7. Serve with a topping of the cheese, orange zest, almonds and paprika.

Tunisian Sweet Potatoes

Prep Time: 15 mins
Total Time: 8 hrs 30 mins

Servings per Recipe: 8
Calories 259.4
Total Fat 8.1g
Cholesterol 0.0mg
Sodium 255.4mg
Total Carbohydrate 42.6g
Protein 7.1g

Ingredients

- 1/2 cup small red beans, soaked for overnight and drained
- 1 large onion, chopped
- 2 large red bell peppers, chopped
- 3 garlic cloves, minced
- 2 tbsp fresh ginger, minced
- 2 lbs yams, peeled and chopped into 1/2-inch cubes
- 3 C. vegetable broth
- 2 large tomatoes, diced
- 1 - 3 jalapeno pepper, minced
- 1/2 tsp salt
- 1/2 tsp ground cumin
- 1/2 tsp ground coriander
- 1/4 tsp ground cinnamon
- 1/4 tsp ground black pepper
- 1/4 C. creamy peanut butter
- 1/4 C. dry roasted peanuts
- 1 lime, cut into wedges

Directions

1. In a crockpot add all the ingredients except the peanut butter, peanuts and lime wedges and gently stir to combine.
2. Set the crockpot on the low settings.
3. Cook, covered for about 8-10 hours.
4. In a bowl, mix together the peanut butter and a little liquid from the beans mixture.
5. Add the peanut butter mixture in the beans mixture and stir to combine.
6. Top the beans mixture with the peanuts and serve with a drizzling of the lime juice.

NORTH AFRICAN
Chicken Thighs

Prep Time: 15 mins
Total Time: 1 hr

Servings per Recipe: 4
Calories 361.4
Total Fat 12.9g
Cholesterol 188.8mg
Sodium 205.9mg
Total Carbohydrate 8.9g
Protein 46.1g

Ingredients

2 lbs boneless skinless chicken thighs
For the Marinade
1 tsp fresh ground black pepper
1 tbsp ground cumin
1 tbsp olive oil
1 medium yellow onion, peeled and finely chopped
1 1/2 tsps paprika
1/2 tsp cayenne pepper
6 garlic cloves, peeled and minced
3 tbsp lemon juice
4 tbsp parsley, minced
1/2 C. white wine
for the garnishing
2 tbsp parsley, chopped
1 lemon, sliced
green olives, sliced

Directions

1. Grease a 13x9-inch roasting pan.
2. In a large bowl, mix together all the marinade ingredients.
3. Add 1/3 of the marinade mixture in the prepared roasting pan.
4. Place the chicken thighs over the marinade and top with the remaining marinade mixture evenly.
5. Refrigerate, covered for at least 1 hour.
6. Set your oven to 350 degrees F.
7. Cook in the oven for about 45 minutes, flipping the chicken thighs occasionally.
8. Serve with a garnishing of the olives, lemon slices and parsley alongside couscous.

Plum Tomato Salad Tunisian

Prep Time: 15 mins
Total Time: 30 mins

Servings per Recipe: 1
Calories 181.5
Total Fat 10.7g
Cholesterol 0.0mg
Sodium 596.7mg
Total Carbohydrate 20.7g
Protein 2.1g

Ingredients

- 8 plum tomatoes, halved, seeded and chopped roughly
- 4 shallots, thinly sliced
- 3 tbsp olive oil
- 4 garlic cloves, minced
- 1 tsp pepper
- 1 tsp ground cumin
- 1 tsp caraway seed
- 1 tsp paprika
- 1/2 tsp turmeric
- 1/3 C. red wine vinegar
- 3 tbsp brown sugar
- 1 tsp salt
- 1 C. fresh cilantro

Directions

1. In a large skillet, heat the oil on medium-high heat and sauté the garlic and seasoning for about 30 seconds.
2. Stir in the sugar, salt and vinegar and boil, stirring continuously for about 3 minutes.
3. Stir in the tomatoes and shallot and cook for about 1-2 minutes.
4. Stir in the cilantro and serve.

TUNISIAN
Puff Pastry
(Brik)

Prep Time: 30 mins
Total Time: 1 hr

Servings per Recipe: 2
Calories 648.6
Total Fat 39.1g
Cholesterol 223.3mg
Sodium 1065.8mg
Total Carbohydrate 34.1g
Protein 38.4g

Ingredients
2 oz. butter, melted
1 small onion, finely chopped
6 1/2 oz. tuna in vegetable oil, drained
1 tbsp capers, rinsed and chopped
2 tbsp flat leaf parsley, finely chopped
2 tbsp parmesan cheese, grated
6 sheets phyllo pastry
2 small eggs

Directions
1. Set your oven to 400 degrees F before doing anything else and lightly, grease a baking dish.
2. For filling in a small frying pan, melt the butter on low heat and sauté the onion for about 5 minutes.
3. In a large bowl, mix together the cooked onion, Parmesan, tuna, capers, parsley, salt and black pepper.
4. Cut the pastry sheets in half in width.
5. Coat the four of the half sheets with the melted butter and place in a layer.
6. Cover the remaining pastry sheets with the damp cloth before using.
7. Place half of the tuna mixture over one end of the buttered pastry, leaving the edges.
8. Make a well in the middle of the filling and carefully, break 1 egg in the well and sprinkle with the salt and black pepper.
9. Place 2 more sheets in a layer and coat with butter.
10. Arrange these 2 buttered sheets over filling and fold the sides and then roll into a parcel, keeping the sides intact.
11. Repeat with the remaining pastry sheets, filling and the egg.
12. Arrange the pastries onto prepared baking dish in a single layer and cook in the oven for about 15 minutes.

Tunisian Couscous Breakfast (Farka)

Prep Time: 15 mins
Total Time: 1 hr 30 mins

Servings per Recipe: 8
Calories 597.0
Total Fat 22.7g
Cholesterol 8.5mg
Sodium 209.6mg
Total Carbohydrate 87.7g
Protein 14.5g

Ingredients

- 2 2/3 C. couscous
- 2 2/3 C. water
- 1/2 C. sugar
- 1/4 C. vegetable oil
- 1 1/2 C. chopped toasted mixed nuts (such as walnuts, blanched almonds, hazelnuts, pistachios and pine nuts)
- 1 (8 oz.) boxes pitted dates, cut into pieces
- 2 C. milk, hot
- additional sugar

Directions

1. In a large heatproof bowl, add the couscous and keep aside.
2. In a heavy pan, add the oil, 1/2 C. sugar and 2 2/3 C. water and cook, stirring continuously till the sugar dissolves.
3. Place the sugar mixture over couscous then stir to combine well and keep aside covered for about 10 minutes.
4. Uncover the bowl and with a fork, fluff the couscous.
5. Add dates and nuts and stir to combine.
6. Transfer the mixture into a 13x9-inch baking dish evenly and keep aside to cool completely.
7. Set your oven to 350 degrees F.
8. Cook in the oven for about 20 minutes.
9. Serve this couscous with hot milk and with a sprinkling of the extra sugar.

ZA'ATAR
Moroccan Spice Mix

Prep Time: 5 mins
Total Time: 5 mins

Servings per Recipe: 2
Calories 367.8
Fat 28.3g
Cholesterol 0.0mg
Sodium 18621.4mg
Carbohydrates 25.4g
Fiber 14.9g
Protein 1.7g

Ingredients

4 tablespoons ground sumac
2 tablespoons whole thyme
3 tablespoons toasted sesame seeds, coarsely ground
2 tablespoons oregano
2 tablespoons ground marjoram
1 teaspoon savory
1 teaspoon basil
2 tablespoons sea salt

Directions

1. Grab a mortar and pestle and add in: sumac, thyme, and sesame.
2. Grind the spices until everything is smooth then add in: the oregano, marjoram, savory, and basil.
3. Continue grinding everything until it is smooth.
4. Now add in the salt and grind everything again.
5. Enjoy.

Ras el Hanout Spice Mix

Prep Time: 5 mins
Total Time: 5 mins

Servings per Recipe: 8
Calories	4 kcal
Carbohydrates	0.8 g
Cholesterol	0 mg
Fat	0.2 g
Fiber	0.3 g
Protein	0.1 g
Sodium	195 mg

Ingredients
- 1 tsp salt
- 1 tsp ground cumin
- 1 tsp ground ginger
- 1 tsp ground turmeric
- 3/4 tsp ground cinnamon
- 3/4 tsp freshly ground black pepper
- 1/2 tsp ground white pepper
- 1/2 tsp ground coriander seed
- 1/2 tsp ground cayenne pepper
- 1/2 tsp ground allspice
- 1/2 tsp ground nutmeg
- 1/4 tsp ground cloves

Directions
1. Combine salt, turmeric, cinnamon, black pepper, ginger, white pepper, coriander, cayenne pepper, cumin, allspice, nutmeg, and cloves in a small sized bowl thoroughly.
2. Store this in a container that is airtight up to 1 month.

Printed in Great Britain
by Amazon